FEMALE GENITAL MUTILATION

FEMALE GENITAL MUTILATION

TREATING THE TEARS

DR HASEENA LOCKHAT

MIDDLESEX
UNIVERSITY
PRESS

First published in 2004 by Middlesex University Press

ISBN   1 898253 90 0

A CIP catalogue record for this book is available from
The British Library

Design by Helen Taylor

Printed and bound in the UK by Hobbs the Printers, Hampshire.

Middlesex University Press would like to thank Banahene Agyemang-Prempeh for allowing us to use his original work of art in the front cover design.

The Figures in Chapter 1 have been reproduced for the purposes of this publication from *FGM: A Teacher's Guide* by the kind permission of **WHO**, Geneva.

Middlesex University Press would like to express thanks to **FORWARD** for their invaluable assistance in the compilation of this book.

Middlesex University Press, Queensway, Enfield, Middlesex EN4 3SF
Tel: +44 (0)20 8411 5734: +44 (0)20 8880 4262 Fax: +44 (0)20 8411 5736
www.mupress.co.uk

To Waqar Azmi

*Thank you for being my source
of inspiration and strength.*

ABOUT THE AUTHOR

DR HASEENA LOCKHAT is a child clinical psychologist at North Warwickshire Primary Care Trust, based at the Lea Castle Centre, Kidderminster. She is a member of the government's Race Equality Advisory Panel (REAP), and also the Community Cohesion Panel (CCP) where she chairs the health and social care sub-group. She is Home Secretary appointee on the National Probation Service (West Mercia Board) and Governor at University College Worcester (UCW).

CONTENTS

FOREWORD

Female Genital Mutilation (FGM) is a collective term for a range of procedures involving partial or total removal of the external female genitalia or other injury to the female genital organs for cultural or other non-therapeutic reasons. It is an extremely painful and harmful practice. Many of its victims are young and vulnerable.

I have visited support groups working with women who have suffered this appalling practice and was very moved by their terrible plight. Victims of this dreadful procedure suffer enormous physical and psychological harm throughout their lives. Regardless of cultural background, the mutilation and impairment of young girls and women have no place in a modern, civilised society.

FGM has been explicitly illegal in this country since 1985 when the Prohibition of Female Circumcision Act was passed. This was an important and welcome step in the fight against FGM. But evidence suggests that people in some communities may be evading our law by taking girls abroad for FGM. The Female Genital Mutilation Bill introduced by Ann Clwyd MP on 11 December 2002 will, if it becomes law, help to close this loophole in the law. It has the Government's full support.

Of course, legislation alone cannot eradicate a practice that has been deeply ingrained in the social fabric of some communities for centuries. Educating communities about the dangers of FGM and the unacceptability of such a brutal practice is the best way to break the cycle of mutilation and suffering.

This book, the culmination of six years' painstaking research, is a valuable exposition of the difficulties faced by both women and girls from the communities who seek to continue this brutal practice and those of us determined to eradicate it.

Rt Hon David Blunkett MP
Home Secretary

INTRODUCTION

I am pleased to have been asked to write an introduction to this interesting, hugely informative and carefully researched book. It also makes recommendations for action needed at local and national level, which the Department of Health will be studying.

There are many aspects to this issue and it is one to be addressed across Government. The Department of Health has a particular role to play. It is doctors, nurses and midwives who deal with the health consequences of FGM and these can be so severe as to last a woman's lifetime.

The key to eradicating FGM is education and therein is the difficulty – accessing close-knit communities who can often be suspicious of officialdom, to persuade them to abandon a practice that has been deeply rooted in their culture and tradition for centuries.

That is why the Department is working closely with FORWARD, the leading organisation in this field. FORWARD has the relevant staff and skills to gain access to the practising communities and work with them on FGM. The Department supports FORWARD financially both in its core activities and for specific FGM projects.

I am sure this book will be of enormous help to health care professionals and policy makers in understanding the complexities of this issue. It will also help raise awareness much more widely.

Melanie Johnson MP
Minister for Public Health

ACKNOWLEDGEMENTS

So many people have been instrumental in helping me to complete this book, and I fear that mere words on a page will not do justice to the immeasurable support and guidance that I have received.

First and foremost, I must thank all the participants of my study – without their help this book would not have been possible. I am indebted to them for putting their trust and confidence in me, for welcoming me into their homes, and for sharing their most personal experiences. From listening to their stories, I have learnt so much about the power of inner strength and courage, as well as the strength and values of family and community support.

I am grateful to Adwoa Kwateng-Kluvitse Director of FORWARD for her expert guidance and constant support; Dr Frank Reeves for copy editing – his painstaking corrections and improvements to my work proved to be a valuable help; Dr Rahmat Mohammad of FORWARD; Zeinab Mohamed, community activist, Manchester; Professor Forest Hansen, Emeritus Professor of Philosophy, Lake Forest College, USA; Maulana Qamaruzzaman Azmi, Secretary General of the World Islamic Mission; Dr Peter Kinderman, Reader in Clinical Psychology, University of Liverpool; and Dr Farhana Lockhat-Clegg, Honorary Clinical Research Fellow, University of Leicester, for all their guidance and helpful comments.

I should also like to acknowledge my thanks to Margaret McKeon, head of child psychology services at the Lea Castle Centre, Kidderminster (North Warwickshire PCT) for her encouragement and support; Dr David Owen, Centre for Research in Ethnic Relations, University of Warwick for providing valuable census data; my wonderful mother, Shirin Lockhat, for her help in proof reading the final manuscript; Professor Colin Francome of Middlesex University Press for keeping a watchful eye during the various stages of this book and Marion Locke, Celia Cozens, Marcella Randall, Elaine Rippington, Denise Arden and the rest of the team from Middlesex University Press for all their hard work in preparing the final manuscript.

My gratitude also goes to the Home Secretary, the Rt Hon David Blunkett for writing the foreword and the Minister for Public Health,

Melanie Johnson for writing the introduction. Immeasurable thanks also to Mark Carroll, Race Equality Adviser to the Permanent Secretary at the Home Office and Jackie Smith, Deputy Minister for Women and Equality at the DTI for their support and assistance.

I wish to thank my family and friends – past and present, for their unconditional support. Finally, this research would never have been undertaken or completed without the encouragement, guidance, and endless patience of my husband, Waqar Azmi. Your intellectual capacity and all round expertise has been invaluable in shaping my ideas throughout this book and your relentless support in helping me achieve my goal, even when at times I was tempted to accept defeat, is truly commendable!

LIST OF TABLES AND FIGURES

TERMS AND TERMINOLOGY

TERMS

Hadith   A saying or action ascribed to the Prophet (pbuh) or an act approved by him

Prophet   The Prophet Muhammad (pbuh), the Messenger of God. Any authority reference to the Prophet is usually followed by the phrase 'peace be upon him (pbuh)'.

Qur'an   The Holy Book of Islam the highest and most authentic authority in Islam. Quotations from the Qur'an are normally followed by a reference to the number of the chapter (sura) and the number of the quoted verse (aya).

Schools of fiqh   The schools of Islamic thought or jurisprudence, the four most important of which were founded by Imam Malik (Malkie), Imam Abu Hanifa (Hanafi), Imam Al-Shafie (Shafie), and Imam Ahmad ibn Hanbal (Hanbalie).

Sharia   The body of Islamic law based on the Qur'an and the sunna (see below).

Sunna   Practices undertaken or approved by the Prophet (pbuh) and established as legally binding precedents.

TERMINOLOGY

1 The terms female genital mutilation (FGM) and female circumcision (FC) are used interchangeably in this book to refer to the practice.

2 The terms Type I *or* mild *or* sunna *or* clitoridectomy; Type II *or* intermediate *or* excision; and Type III *or* severe *or* infibulation *or* pharaonic, are used interchangeably to describe the type of circumcision.

꧁

INTRODUCTION

MY STUDENT DAYS AT THE UNIVERSITY OF MANCHESTER, as for many other people, were blessed with friends from different ethnic and cultural backgrounds, many of whom were from parts of Africa and Southeast Asia where female circumcision (FC), or Female Genital Mutilation (FGM) as it is controversially labelled, is a common cultural practice. This brought me closer to the Sudanese and Somali communities settled in the urban areas of Moss Side and Longsight in south Manchester. Through talking to women, mingling in social and community events, listening to their feelings, opinions, wisdom, and experiences, I learned much about their perspectives and became conscious of the 'triple jeopardy' that they were facing in the UK – for being *black, female,* and *circumcised!* I witnessed not only the extreme xenophobic attitudes towards them but also the degree of ignorance by health care practitioners about their predicament. It was shocking to see how little information and knowledge local authorities and health bodies had about these communities. It was clear to me that this only exacerbated the sufferings of these women.

Against this background I decided to devote my Clinical Psychology Doctorate thesis to this topic. My aim at the outset, as it has been for this book, was first to help women and girls who suffer physical and psychological complications as a result of their circumcision, and second, to help health and social care providers and practitioners who, for the first time, may be encountering conditions in women that result from circumcision.

Female circumcision is not a new phenomenon. It has existed throughout history in many parts of the world, including the UK. The practice, however, ceased to exist in the UK and elsewhere in the West by the late 19th century. In the 1980s, however, it resurfaced and attracted media attention when it became known that some private clinics in London were performing circumcision on girls and women from overseas. Whilst this triggered the government to bring in what was then the Prohibition of Female Circumcision Act (1985) to prevent health professionals from carrying out these procedures, it did not eliminate the practice. The devastation of civil war and famine in certain parts of Africa at the same period brought greater number of refugees, asylum seekers and economic migrants who continued with their cultural practice either illegally or abroad, since the Act did not prohibit children from being taken out of the country for the purpose of circumcision.

Whilst the UK as a member state of the UN has been at the forefront of bringing legislative measures, ratifying, for example, the UN Convention on the Elimination of all forms of Discrimination Against Women (CEDAW) 1979, the Convention on the Rights of the Child (CRC) 1990, and the Beijing Declaration and Platform for Action (1995), it has failed to take a holistic approach to eliminate the practice and to ensure the physical and mental wellbeing of those girls and women experiencing circumcision. To its credit the UK did recognise FGM as a denial of a child's basic human right and classified the practice as a form of child abuse by incorporating it as a special concern into 'Working Together under the Children's Act (1989) – A Guide for Inter-Agency Co-operation for the Protection of Children from Abuse', and again in the updated version 'Working Together to Safeguard Children' (1999), which was a joint publication by the Department of Health (DoH), Home Office (HO), and the then Department for Education and Employment (DfEE).

One can justifiably be forgiven for seeing these as pure 'cosmetic dressings', however, as the UK still has no effective procedure either to identify girls 'at risk' or to identify those that have been taken away to be circumcised. In addition, there is no blanket training, information, or guidance to health providers and health professionals, and few support mechanisms for girls who have suffered from their experience. This was raised by Baroness Gould, who tabled a motion in the House of Lords back in 1998 which reflected the views of peers who were also concerned over the lack of progress on the issue in terms of education, prevention, and prosecution.

This is not to say that there are no positive local initiatives in the UK. There are several, and I have been moved by the selfless efforts of many women, men, and community groups working day and night in parts of the country. However, their efforts are largely unsupported, their initiatives lack funding, and their work often goes unrecognised.

There is a real opportunity for their work to be co-ordinated, for good practice to be shared and a real difference to be made. There is also an opportunity to learn from elsewhere, as I did during my visits to Egypt, Kenya, and the Gambia, where co-ordinated efforts involving local religious and community leaders are helping to eliminate the centuries-old cultural practice.

Research biography and methods

This book is a product of over six years of research carried out in two phases. Phase one was for my doctorate thesis between 1997 and 1999. Phase two was for this book between 2000 and 2003. Doing research usually involves painstaking procedures, made greater by the sensitive nature of the subject, reluctance of people to talk, full-time employment and other professional and personal commitments. It certainly presents the individual researcher with a mammoth task and can become a way of life as one's life becomes woven into the research just as much as the research becomes part of one's life.

Demands on the emotions are certainly felt very acutely where one is working in such fields. For example, it is very difficult to keep calm while listening to colleagues and professionals airing their views on how these women are a drain on the NHS. The researcher in a locality cannot remain isolated. She is a resource that individuals and groups within the locality try to utilise – families ask for help in understanding letters from the local authority, or for advice on reversal operations. Such simple aid cannot be refused; but when one is invited to state opinions and express support about local issues, it raises the questions of how detached the researcher should be. With the daily comings and goings of community life go friendships, and with friendships go invitations to meet families and friends. All these are good research opportunities, but they are also opportunities to become a participant non-observer in the life of the women.

To avoid sentimentality, however, it is best only to indicate those personal experiences where they impinge upon the methodology. Both phases of the research involved a combination of methods. Interviews were held with fifty-five circumcised women living in the areas of Moss Side and Longsight in south Manchester to gauge their physical and psychological experiences as well as their perceptions, views and experiences of the health and social care services in the UK. Forty-five women had experienced severe type circumcision and ten had experienced the mild form of circumcision. Four focus groups were held involving fifty people and thirty one-to-one interviews were held with key individuals such as campaigners and leading religious officials. Observational visits to the Gambia, Kenya and Egypt were made between 1999-2003, and for chapter three on female circumcision in Islam, group discussions were held with African Muslim families to identify key issues. Over the course of the research several conferences, functions and consultation meetings and a number of informal discussion groups organised by bodies such as FORWARD and the SWITCH project were attended, and analyses and reviews of secondary research findings, reports, books, policies and legislative frameworks were undertaken. Names of the participants are not identified in adherence to their requests – with the exception of those that gave specific permissions.

The structure of this book

This book is divided into eleven chapters. Chapter one defines FGM and the various forms it takes. It explores the history of FGM, looking at reasons why it is carried out and various methods used to circumcise girls and women. It also shows current prevalence rates worldwide, outlining the geographical distribution in terms of countries where it continues to be practised.

Chapter two touches upon the controversial debate around human rights versus human rites. Whilst opponents of the practice agitate for its global elimination as it violates basic human rights, proponents campaign equally for its maintenance on the grounds of cultural relativism and the right for centuries-old customs and traditions to exist. Many countries in recent times have acknowledged the human rights stance over and above cultural maintenance arguments and signed up to international conventions or even outlawed the practice. However, most of them face a barrage of criticism from their citizens for bowing to western influence. For them, the West is a hypocritical, white, racist group of nations that allows face-lifts, breast enhancement or reduction, rib reduction, and sex change operations to happen routinely, yet abhors and condemns cultural practices such as female circumcision.

Over the years the practice of FGM has increasingly come to be linked to religious obligatory practices – particularly Islam. El-Dareer (1983a) pointed out that this is evident from various attitudinal surveys that have investigated why people insist upon the practice. Modesty and chastity are used to justify the practice by many who carry it out, as endorsed by some religious leaders. The popular assumption that FGM is an Islamic practice may also be due to the fact that the pharaonic-type circumcision, which is the severest type, is mainly practised in countries where Islam is the principal religion. Chapter three, therefore, looks at female circumcision in Islam. It explores what Islam says about the practice, where the Islamic *Sharia* (divine law) stands on this issue, and what the views of leading Islamic *ulemas* and scholars are.

Worldwide prevalence of FGM is estimated to affect about 140 million women, with an additional two million girls and women undergoing the procedure every year. The practice is prevalent in more than twenty-six African countries and among a few minority groups in Southeast Asia. In African countries this varies widely from about 5 per cent in Uganda and the Democratic Republic of Congo (former Zaire), to 98 per cent in Somalia. In addition, many immigrant women in Europe, Canada, and the United States have undergone FGM. Some estimate 15 per cent of all circumcised women to have undergone the most severe infibulation-type. Chapters four and five survey this international scene and act as a reference point on the issue of female circumcision globally. The chapters provide a general account of prevalence rates, action on eradication, and current legislation in a number of FGM-practising countries. They also look at the situation in Europe, Canada and the United States and explore the various international conventions and declarations protecting the rights of women and children, as well as calling for appropriate and effective measures by individual states to eradicate the practice

Chapter six focuses on FGM in the UK. It illustrates how female circumcision prevailed in the UK, receiving wide acceptance and endorsement by the church up until the end of the nineteenth century. It then disappeared only to resurface in the 1980s following the arrival of immigrants, asylum seekers, and refugees from FGM-practising countries (such as Somalia, Sudan, Djibouti, Eritrea, Ethiopia, Sierra Leone, and Nigeria). The chapter looks at the settlements and demographic patterns of these groups in the UK, legislative developments, non-governmental organisation (NGO) initiatives, local responses, and the work of professional bodies in tackling the issue.

Chapters seven, eight and nine are based on a qualitative study carried out in the urban areas of south Manchester with women of Sudanese and Somali communities and are a powerful recording of the perceptions and views of many women who have experienced FGM (Lockhat, 1999). Chapter seven documents the physical problems circumcised women have experienced throughout their lives. For many women, the most difficult physical problems experienced coincide with various lifecycle events, such as immediately post-circumcision, at menstruation, at the time of marriage and during childbirth.

Chapter eight focuses on women's psychological experiences. Whilst numerous studies have been done to assess the potential physical impact of FGM, far less has been done with regards to psychological and emotional consequences. This is due partly to difficulties in measuring psychological distress, and partly to women's reluctance to discuss these issues. Many assumptions have, therefore, been made about the likely effects of circumcision on women's psychological and emotional well-being. Whilst there have been reports of phobic reactions, chronic irritability, fear of sexual relations, loss of self esteem, feelings of victimisation, severe anxiety prior to the operation and depression and sexual frustration, there have also been contradictory findings indicating an absence of psychopathology (Burstyn, 1995; Toubia, 1994; Arbesman, Kahler and Buck, 1993; Lightfoot-Klein 1989; Omen, 1983; Basher, 1977; 1982; Mahran, 1981; Verzin, 1977). An absence of concrete data makes it difficult to provide mental health and social care services to help and support circumcised women, as there is uncertainty as to the extent of support women need, and what the best way is of providing this.

The chapter aims to fill this gap by shedding light on the kinds of psychological problems circumcised women living in this country are experiencing. It looks at women's subjective recollection of their circumcision experience, the nature of their psychological and emotional distress, prevalence rates of clinical psychopathology amongst the sample of women, and addresses predictors in the development of clinical psychopathology.

Chapter nine explores women's experiences of health and social care in the UK. Most women in the study had bad experiences with health and social care services in this country. For many, the experience not only tainted their views and attitudes towards health professionals, but was also an important determinant in the development of psychopathology. Some accounts are shocking but not surprising, given that little preparation is available for health care providers and professionals on how to meet the needs of circumcised women effectively.

Chapters ten and eleven deal with the important topic of how to work with and care for circumcised women. Most health professionals have no knowledge or understanding of the issue. Others do not see it as a problem in this country. Yet the stakes are high, particularly when quick decisions have to be made in emergency situations. Whilst some guidelines or position papers have been issued by the government and other professional bodies, these are sparse and lack the 'hands on' guidance and information that professionals desperately need when confronted with the issue in practice.

Finally, a host of recommendations are put forward for action and improvements needed at local and national levels to help those who have been circumcised as well as those who care for them, and to ensure the elimination of the practice.

CHAPTER ONE

HISTORY OF
FEMALE CIRCUMCISION

Introduction

This chapter explains what female circumcision is, its various types, history and origin. It outlines the reasons why it is carried out in parts of Africa and Southeast Asia and the various methods used to circumcise girls and women. The chapter also looks at the current prevalence rates worldwide and the geographical distribution. Finally, it explains the main differences between female and male circumcision.

What is female circumcision?

'Female circumcision' is a term given to traditional practices involving the intentional cutting of or partial or total removal of the external female genitalia (WHO 1997). The main difference between male and female circumcision, as will be discussed later in this chapter, is that when males undergo circumcision only the outer skin of the penis is removed without touching the penis itself. In contrast, there are certain types of female circumcision, which involve extensive removal of the female genitalia. For this reason many argue that the term 'female genital mutilation' (FGM) is a more fitting description of the practice and should be used when referring to the procedure. This, however, is surrounded by controversy and is rejected by those who do not perceive the process to be mutilating. Chapter two provides an insight into this debate.

Types of circumcision

The World Health Organisation (WHO) defines FGM as:

> *all procedures which involve partial or total removal of the external female genitalia or other injury to the female genital organs whether for cultural or any other non-therapeutic reasons*

> WHO, 1997

It categorises the various types as follows (see also figure 1):

Type I: Excision of the prepuce with or without excision of part or all of the clitoris (also known as 'mild' or 'clitoridectomy' or 'sunna' type).

Type II: Excision of the prepuce and clitoris together with partial or total excision of the labia minora (also known as 'intermediate' type).

Type III: Excision of part or all of the external genitalia and stitching/narrowing of the vaginal opening (also known as 'severe' or 'infibulation' or 'pharaonic' type).

Type IV: Unclassified: includes pricking, piercing or incision of clitoris and/or labia; stretching of clitoris and/or labia; cauterisation by burning of clitoris and surrounding tissues; scraping (angurya cuts) of the vaginal orifice or cutting (gishiri cuts) of the vagina; introduction of corrosive substances into the vagina to cause bleeding or herbs into the vagina with the aim of tightening or narrowing the vagina; any other procedure which falls under the definition of FGM given above.

WHO, 1997

The origins of female circumcision

Daly (1950), a psychoanalytical writer, has described how all people have passed through a phase in the evolution of their culture, in which circumcision for both sexes has existed. Whilst there is no conclusive evidence to indicate when and where the custom of female circumcision started and how it spread, historians have traced it back to as early as the fifth century before the Christian era (BCE). The oldest known source that records the custom is the work of Herodotus (484-424 BCE), who states that excision was practised by the Phoenicians, Hittites, and Ethiopians as well as by Egyptians. It is believed to have been carried out as a means of protection against rape for young girls taking animals out to pasture, or as some early attempt at population control (Bilotti, 2000).

Infibulation (Type III), which constitutes the most extreme form of circumcision, derives its name from the Latin word 'fibula', which

Figure 1: Types of FGM

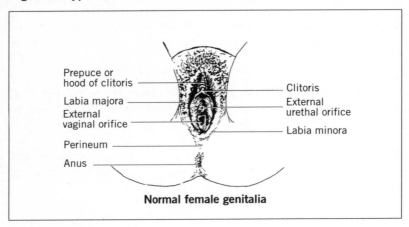

Normal female genitalia

Type I

Exision of the prepuce (the fold of skin above the clitoris) with the tip of the clitoris

Type I may consist of removal of the prepuce without damage to the clitoris

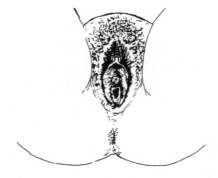

Type I

Exision of the prepuce and clitoris

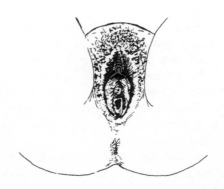

Type II
Exision of the prepuce, clitoris
and labia minora

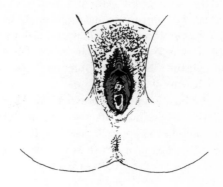

Type III
Infibulated genitalia

    Excised areas

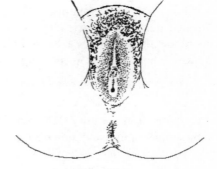

Type IV
Pulled labia minora

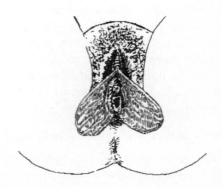

was the name given to the pin used to clasp the Roman toga. The fibula was used to prevent sexual intercourse amongst slaves, thus preventing males from tiring themselves, and also to protect against child bearing which would hinder their work. Fibulas were therefore fastened through the labia majora of female slaves, and/or through the prepuce of male slaves.

Infibulation is also known as `pharaonic circumcision', because it is believed to have been practised during the Pharaohs dynasties (2850-525 BCE) amongst Egyptian females of the ruling class, who were restricted from inheriting property if they were not circumcised (Shandall, 1967).

In the medical literature, ideas about clitoridectomy on medical grounds appeared as early as 138 CE. Soramus, a Greek physician in Alexandria and Rome, described in detail the instruments he used to cut away the excess when presented with a large clitoris. Similarly, the physician Aetius (502-575 CE) described his practice of clitoral amputations using forceps (Hosken, 1993).

The earliest description of infibulation in modern historical literature is that of the Venetian Pietro Bembo in the sixteenth century. In his report on the Red Sea, he described inhabitants of this area of Africa as holding virginity in such high esteem that the

private parts of girls are sewn together immediately after birth
Hosken, 1994

In the eighteenth century, following the refusal by African-born Catholic converts to marry non-excised women, Catholic missionaries condoned the practice of female circumcision as sanctioned by the Papacy of the Roman Catholic Church on the basis that non-excision was deplorable to men and thus a hindrance to marriage.

There is no consensus as to whether the practice of female circumcision and the different forms it takes originated in one locality and then spread elsewhere, or was practised by different ethnic groups in different areas at different times. Two main theories have been put forward regarding this. The first suggests that it began in one place (the Arabian peninsula or Egypt) and spread to other parts. The second argues that the widespread nature of the practice makes it more likely that it developed independently in different places at different periods in history (Bilotti, 2000)

Current prevalence and geographical distribution

World Health Organisation figures estimate 140 million cases of female circumcision world wide, with approximately two million females at risk of the practice each year (WHO, 1998). FGM is practised in more than twenty-six countries of the African continent (see figure 2 and Chapters four and five for detailed discussions), and in some areas of the Arabian Peninsula and Southeast Asia. Whilst the focus of this book is on Types I, II and III, it should be noted that Type IV circumcision is currently reported to be sweeping across parts of Africa and, particularly, Nigeria. It is fast becoming the 'new fad' in the business of circumcision, particularly in the form that involves tightening or narrowing the vagina through the use of herbs. This type of circumcision reportedly increases friction during sexual intercourse, thus enhancing sexual pleasure for some males. This type of intercourse is more commonly known as 'dry sex'. However, it is currently not taken seriously as a form of FGM and little is known about its prevalence and extent around the world.

The practice of FGM today is not solely a characteristic of non-western societies, since mobility, through immigration and asylum, has brought the practice to Europe and the USA. This will be discussed in detail in chapter four.

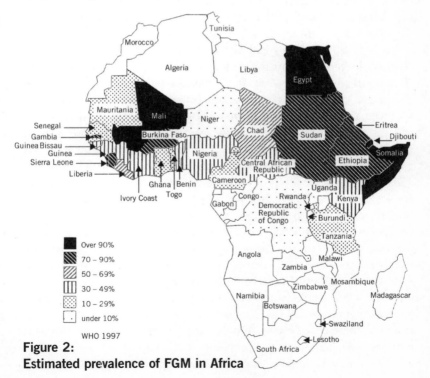

Figure 2:
Estimated prevalence of FGM in Africa

Age and procedure

The age at which girls and women are circumcised varies greatly, from shortly after birth to after childbirth, in accordance with geographical location and the prevailing local customs and culture.

More often, traditional birth attendants, local (often elderly) women of the village or a member of the family, perform the circumcision. For many, the operation constitutes a lucrative source of income. In Mali and Senegal it tends to be carried out by women of the blacksmith caste gifted with knowledge of the occult. In Sudan, Somalia, and Egypt, it tends to be done by untrained midwives. In the more urban areas of some countries where the practice is not outlawed, it is not uncommon nowadays, for it to be performed in hospitals by medical professionals.

Instruments used to perform the operation include household knives, sharp stones, broken glass, old razor blades (Woodlard et al, 1997), and scalpels in hospital settings (Slack, 1988). Instruments are rarely sterilised before, during or after the operation, and are often used to carry out multiple operations. Anaesthesia (except in some urban areas) is seldom used (Jordan, 1994; Ntiri, 1993; Lightfoot-Klein & Shaw, 1991) and incisions are usually made with the girl lying on the floor, being held down by several women (Minority Rights Group, 1996). Wounds are typically covered with local herbs, eggs, ash, vaseline, mud, or dung to stop the bleeding. In infibulation-type operations in which the entire clitoris, labia minora, and much of the labia majora are removed, the edges of raw flesh are then fused together with acacia tree thorns, stitches, cat gut, or adhesives made from egg and sugar, so that the entire area is closed up except for a tiny opening which is preserved by the insertion of a reed, twig, straw, or match into the incision to allow for the flow of urine and menstrual blood (Arbesman, Kahler and Buck, 1993). The whole procedure takes from fifteen to twenty minutes, depending on the ability of the operator and the child's resistance (Mustafa, 1966). The girl's legs are then tightly bound together in order to heal the area, which can take from fifteen to forty days (de Villeneuve, 1937). During this time, movement is restricted and special foods believed to assist with the healing, are prepared.

The level of celebration accompanying the practice varies greatly amongst countries and cultures. In some areas, as in parts of Sudan for example, there may be days of preparation during which the house is redecorated, elaborate feasts prepared, family and friends invited from afar, with much singing and dancing. The whole event is one of excitement, anticipation, and festivity. The girl is showered with gifts, money, and new clothes, adorned with henna and gold jewellery, and given almost bride-like status (Basher, 1977). In other areas, as in parts of Somalia, however, the operation is carried out merely as a routine activity with no ceremony or celebration.

Practice at the time of marriage also varies cross-culturally. In some cases the infibulation is gradually enlarged as a consequence of months of penile thrusting (Lantier, 1972). In other cases the husband may use his fingers, a razor, or knife to open the scar. In parts of Somalia, women visit the midwife around the time of marriage to be de-infibulated (to have the scar opened) to a point enabling penetration to occur. Cultural variation also occurs following childbirth. In some parts of Sudan for example, women are commonly re-infibulated following delivery – such that the vaginal opening is tightened to resemble the original circumcision (Khalifa, 1994; Lightfoot-Klein, 1989b). Re-circumcision (re-infibulation) was not a common practice until early this century and is believed to have been a practice that spread from educated women in urban areas (El Dareer, 1983a).

Reasons for the practice of FGM

A whole host of reasons are given to explain why FGM is carried out. Some of the key ones are outlined below:

Tradition

Tradition accounts for the most widely held justification for the practice of female circumcision which follows generations of culturally embedded beliefs. In many groups, circumcision signifies the passage into adulthood and thus serves as an initiation rite and a prerequisite to acceptance and belonging. Social acceptance is important to most African families and social ostracism is avoided at all cost, even if it means embracing a practice that inflicts pain and suffering.

Religion

Although carried out by Muslims, Jews, Christians (Catholics, Protestants, Copts), and atheists, the practice of female circumcision predates both Islam and Christianity. Whilst three religions (Islam, Judaism and Christianity) discuss male circumcision, none require the practice for females. Nevertheless, over the years the practice has erroneously been linked to religious obligatory rites, particularly Islam, as is evident from various surveys that have investigated why people insist upon the practice (El-Dareer 82). This can largely be attributed to advocacy by some religious leaders, who cite modesty and chastity as clear justifiable reasons for the practice. Such misguided interpretation of religious values, instils a sense of fear and compliance of the practice. In addition, pharaonic type circumcision, which is the severest form and which consequently receives the most media and public attention, tends to be more widely carried out in countries in which Islam is the principal religion. Misconception that it is an Islamic practice clearly comes to light, however, when one realises that Christians, Jews and those of other religions residing in these countries also carry out the ritual (Toubia, 1994). Furthermore, when one considers that the practice does not prevail and is much condemned in countries such as Saudi Arabia, the centre of the Islamic world, it becomes clear that the notion that it is an Islamic practice is a false one (see chapter three for more detail). This indeed was one of the aims of an extensive report written by Pridie et al (1945), which included a statement by Sheikh Ahmed El Taher, Mufti of Sudan, in which circumcision was condemned on religious grounds. Nevertheless, half a century later the practice still prevails under the pretext of religious obligation.

Preservation of chastity

Another interpretation, and one that has transcended time, culture, and civilisation, is that circumcision ensures virginity, preserves the chastity of a woman, and thus maintains family honour (Assaad, 1979). Amongst many groups who practice circumcision, preservation of virginity is of paramount importance and determines a woman's position in society. Within some communities, the value of a prospective bride is based on the size of the infibulated opening – the smaller it is, the more valuable her worth. This is believed not only to ensure virginity, but also to enhance a woman's femininity, increase male sexual satisfaction because of the tightness of the vagina and attenuate female sexual desire – rendering her less vulnerable to sexual temptation (Hathout, 1963). Since the clitoris is believed to drive women into making uncontrollable, insatiable demands for sex which their husbands may not be able to satisfy, removal of this organ is believed to minimise promiscuity and the likelihood of extra-marital affairs, whilst not interfering with reproductive abilities. It is believed to be of benefit not only to the woman herself, but also to the wider society.

Myths and superstitions

Justification for the practice is also based on a number of mythical beliefs passed down over many generations. One myth which upholds the tradition of both male and female circumcision goes back to the pharaonic belief in the bisexuality of the Gods, and the belief that the foreskin in males represents the feminine soul in the male, whilst the clitoris in females represents the male soul in females.According to the myth, adolescents cannot enter into adulthood until opposite sex characteristics have been removed. If the clitoris is not removed, some believe it can cause male impotence.

In some communities, circumcision occurs when women are in advanced stages of pregnancy, in accordance with the myth that the infant will die if its head touches the clitoris during childbirth.Another myth claims that if left intact, the clitoris will cause symbolic or spiritual injury to the baby, or release a poisonous substance that kills babies during childbirth (Myers et al, 1985). Some even believe that the clitoris represents the male sex organ, which if not removed will grow to the size of a penis (Nayra, 1982). Others believe that excision is necessary to enhance a woman's fertility and that a non-excised woman will be barren.

Socio-economic reasons

Other possible explanations have considered the early pharaonic tradition of inheritance of title and kinship, which was through the mother not the father. Female circumcision may have been a means of ensuring the legitimacy of claims (Burstyn, 1995). In many countries, culture dictates that females left uncircumcised are, to an extent, ostracised from the community and left socially isolated and in poverty. Since proof of virginity remains a pre-requisite to marriage and inheritance of property, the socio-economic cost to families leaving their daughters uncircumcised is high, since the husband has the right to reject an uncircumcised woman, and to refuse to continue with the marriage. Some Somali men living in the UK, for example, have been known to refuse marriage to uncircumcised women (Shaw, 1985). Female circumcision is also an important source of income for those involved in carrying out the practice. As such, these individuals have a vested interest in perpetuating the practice (Shaw, 1985) and often use their status as an elder in the community to encourage others to get it done for their daughters.

Pursuit of hygiene

In some countries the female external genitalia are considered unclean and productive of a harmful and offensive odour. Women are believed to be naturally polluted and can only reach a state of cleanliness suitable for marriage and childbirth through excision (Hosken, 1994). This reasoning seems ironic, given that circumcision often gives rise to infection and subsequent odours.

Aesthetic reasons

In addition to these longstanding cultural and traditional beliefs, more recently, circumcision has been carried out at the request of women for cosmetic reasons – e.g. usually because they or their partner think their labia are ugly (Koso-Thomas, 1987).

Curative reasons

In Europe and America, forms of circumcision were carried out to treat psychosocial disorders (Sequeira, 1931). Britain in the 1800s saw clitoridectomy widely advocated as a cure for insanity, epilepsy, masturbation, lesbianism, hysteria (Toubia, 1994), and nymphomania (Burstyn, 1995) (see chapter six for further depth).

Other

Other reasons include demands for the practice by women themselves. Although widely claimed that the operation is performed because of male demands, it is more often the women who demand that it continues, and ensure that it is done. Perhaps one unspoken reason why they themselves perpetuate it with such force despite the pain, suffering, and adverse physical and mental consequences which they themselves have endured, is their quest for others to have to experience what they have had to. Shandall's study of female circumcision in Sudan found 35 per cent of women had insisted on the practice for their own children and grandchildren for this reason:

> *If I submitted to this and bore it, then so shall those who follow*
> Shandall 1967

Why female circumcision is different to male circumcision

As mentioned earlier, circumcision for both sexes has existed throughout history. Among those who have studied the origins of male circumcision (MC) such as Wrana (1939), Bitschai (1956), and Wallerstein (1980), there is a consensus that its roots originated thousands of years ago, pre-dating Islam, Christianity and Judaism, with depictions of circumcision found even in Stone-Age cave drawings. Tribal identification, rites of initiation, and fertility rituals were considered the primary purpose of male circumcision. The practice existed in many parts of Africa and was unknown to the Romans until they conquered Egypt and the Middle East. In a number of Western countries the practice of male circumcision for non-religious reasons became prevalent by the beginning of the twentieth century. Within the miasma of myth and ignorance (when the aetiology of most diseases was unknown), a theory emerged that masturbation caused many and varied ills. It seemed logical to some physicians to perform genital surgery to both sexes to stop this.

In 1891, Dr P Remondino advocated circumcision to prevent or cure alcoholism, epilepsy, asthma, hernia, gout, rheumatism, curvature of the spine and headaches (Remondino, 1891). Gellis (1978) points out that male circumcision took a boost during the Second World War because it helped to minimise wartime 'hygiene problems'. In the 1930s circumcision was thought to prevent cancer of the penis (Wolbarst, 1932). Schoen (1990) pointed out that up until the late 1950s middle-class parents in the USA always circumcised their newborn sons whilst infants from poor, impoverished backgrounds were uncircumcised because their parents were either not able to afford the practice or to understand the benefits.

Male circumcision, however, continues to be the most common surgical operation in the modern day world. Yet it is free from much controversy and does not attract the level of prohibitive measures globally as does female circumcision. It is practised by Jews, Muslims and people of other faiths as well as those of no faith throughout the world. Although numbers have fallen, particularly in Britain, in other parts of Europe and America, millions of male infants are still circumcised every day. Some have estimated that between 25 and 35 per cent of Australian male infants and 50 and 75 per cent of American male infants are circumcised (Little, 1992 and Schoen, 1990).

The key difference, however, between male and female circumcision is that male circumcision involves the removal of the foreskin, or prepuce, from the penis without touching the penis itself. By contrast, female circumcision comprises partial or total removal of the external female genitalia and can cause a total loss of stimulation and sexual desire, even in its mildest form. This difference is explicitly defined by Toubia:

> *The degree of cutting in female circumcision is anatomically much more extensive. The male equivalent of clitoridectomy (in which all or part of the clitoris is removed) would be the amputation of most of the penis. The male equivalent of infibulation (which involves not only clitoridectomy, but also the removal or closing off of the sensitive tissue around the vagina) would be removal of the entire penis, its roots of soft tissue, and part of the scrotal skin.*
>
> Toubia, 1993

There are also stark differences in motivation behind male and female circumcision. Reasons given for female circumcision have been outlined previously. Male circumcision is generally carried out for reasons of religion, as in the Jewish and Muslim faiths, where it is practised in accordance with Abraham's covenant with God. Others carry it out for reasons of hygiene or aesthetics. Furthermore, unlike female circumcision, male circumcision is not performed for reasons of chastity or to preserve virginity, nor with the intention of diminishing male sexual desire or drive.

CHAPTER TWO

HUMAN RIGHTS
VERSUS
HUMAN RITES

Introduction

This chapter looks at the controversial debate around human rights versus human rites. Opponents of the practice of FC agitate for its global elimination as it violates basic human rights, whilst proponents campaign for its maintenance on grounds of cultural relativism and the right for centuries-old customs and traditions to exist. Many countries have, in recent times, acknowledged the human rights stance over and above cultural maintenance arguments and signed up to international conventions or even outlawed the practice. However, most of them face a barrage of criticism from their citizens for bowing to western influence. For them, the West is a hypocritical, white, racist group of nations that allow face-lifts, breast enlargement/reduction, rib reduction, and sex changes to happen routinely, yet abhor and condemn cultural practices such as FC.

A human rights issue?

FGM has become a controversial issue. From a western or non-African perspective, it is regarded as a backward, cruel, unthinkable practice. Those opposing the practice argue that it should be eradicated globally, not only because of the detrimental effect it has on women's health and well-being, but also because they refute reasons that are put forward to justify its continuation. They argue, for example, that there is no evidence of it being a fundamental requirement to any religious doctrine. The argument of likely immorality in an absence of the practice is refuted, as infibulation does not guarantee against this. Those wanting to have sexual relations prior to marriage can conceal their act by being re-infibulated. Those who cite negative repercussions of *not* being circumcised to the health of women themselves, to their husbands during intercourse, and to their babies during childbirth have been uncovered as mythical concoctions. Nevertheless, advocates of the practice cling to their beliefs, justifying their right to preserve cultural traditions.

At what point, then, does a practice cease to be accepted on the grounds of tradition and become a violation of human rights justifying external interference? We will first examine key points put forward by those opposing the practice, and then look at arguments of proponents.

Those in opposition to the practice have, over the years, sought to bring the issue into the human rights arena by examining various conventions that they believe can be applied wholeheartedly to FGM. Some of these include:

➡ The Universal Declaration of Human Rights, adopted by the UN General Assembly in December 1948

This asserts that all human beings are born free and equal in dignity and rights. It contains within it a number of articles which are of direct relevance to FGM including:

Article 3:   *Everyone has the right to life, liberty and the security of person.*

Article 5:   *No one shall be subjected to torture or to cruel, inhuman, or degrading treatment or punishment.*

Article 15: *Everyone has the right to a standard of living adequate for the health and well-being of himself.*

➡ The African Charter on Human and People's Rights, adopted in 1981 by the Assembly of Heads of States and in 1990 by the African Organisation of Unity.

The Charter contains several articles which can be related directly to FGM including:

Article 5:   *All forms of exploitation and degradation of man particularly slavery, slave trade, torture, cruel, inhuman or degrading punishment or treatment shall be prohibited.*

Article 16: *Every individual shall have the right to enjoy the best attainable state of physical and mental health.*

Article 18: *The State shall ensure the elimination of every discrimination against women and also ensure the protection of the rights of the women and the child as stipulated in international declarations and conventions.*

In the context of the above, FGM is seen by opponents to be in breach of three key aspects, firstly, the rights to health, secondly the rights of women, and thirdly, the rights of the child. These will be looked at in turn.

Violation of the rights to health

Most countries that practice FGM are third world countries where medical facilities are scant. Even in countries boasting high standards of medical care with state of the art medical equipment, unnecessary operations are contraindicated. Opponents of the practice argue that FGM not only fits into the category of an unnecessary operation, but also indicate poor standards of health care available in these countries, which mean that women and girls are operated upon in unsanitary conditions without proper anaesthetic, and often by untrained individuals using primitive instruments such as broken glass or old knives. This undoubtedly is a highly painful experience, which many have labelled as torturous and which in itself can be categorised as a violation to rights. In addition, it can lead to both immediate and long-term severe and chronic health problems including complications at childbirth. The violation, therefore, is considered to be twofold: violation of the right to health and, in many cases, violation of the rights to life from the perspective of reproduction. The right to enjoy the highest attainable standard of physical and mental health is referred to in the following covenant:

➡ International Covenant on Economic, Social and Cultural Rights (ICESCR 1976)

The covenant proclaims the right to physical and mental health in article 12 which upholds:

the right of everyone to the enjoyment of the highest attainable standard of physical and mental health.

Violation of women's rights

From a feminist perspective it is argued that FGM denies females their sexual integrity, and under a number of conventions there are calls for an end to gender discrimination:

➡ The UN Convention on the Elimination of all forms of Discrimination Against Women (CEDAW 1979)

Article 5 upholds the need to:

modify the social and cultural patterns of conduct of men and women, with a view to achieving the elimination of prejudices and customs and all other practices which are based on the idea of the inferiority or the superiority of either of the sexes or on stereotyped roles for men and women.

➡ **The UN Beijing Declaration and Platform for Action (1995)**

The declaration clearly condemns FGM as a form of violence against women, reaffirming state responsibility to:

condemn violence against women and refrain from invoking any custom, tradition or religious consideration to avoid their obligations with respect to its elimination as set out in the Declaration on the Elimination of Violence against Women.

It defines violence against women as:

any act of gender-based violence that results in, or is likely to result in, physical, sexual or psychological harm or suffering to women, including threats of such acts, coercion or arbitrary deprivation of liberty, whether occurring in public or private life.

Rights of the child

Opponents of the practice argue that any form of FGM practised on children constitutes a violation of the rights of that child and some go as far as to classify FGM in the same league as child abuse. They cite not only general human rights conventions to support their view, but also those that have a specific regard for the welfare of children. These include:

➡ **The Declaration of the Rights of the Child**, adopted in 1959 by the General Assembly of the UN

This declaration states in Article 2 that:

The child shall enjoy specific protection and shall be given opportunities and facilities by law and other means, to enable him to develop physically, mentally, morally, spiritually and socially in a healthy and normal manner and in conditions of freedom and dignity.

Article 12 upholds the:

rights of the child to the enjoyment of the highest attainable standards of health and to medical and rehabilitation facilities.

It also emphasises the need to:

diminish infant and child mortality through appropriate measures.

Freedom to practise human rites?

The difficulty with the conventions outlined above, however, is that they do not clearly condemn the practice. They refer to a need to protect against:

> *inhumane and degrading punishment ... the right to a standard of living adequate for the health and well-being of himself ...* and to protect from *... social and economic exploitation.*

Advocators of the practice argue that FGM is done to uphold all these principles, and that outsiders see it out of context, rather than in relation to their wider culture. They argue that it is not inhumane or degrading or done to exploit or damage health and well-being, but with due regard to the girl's future well-being in mind, so that she is considered eligible for marriage, accepted in her community and the wider society, and is socially and economically secure.

In Kenya, for example, where both males and females are routinely circumcised as a symbol of adulthood, the words of the ex-Kenyan president strike a chord with many proponents of the practice:

> *No proper Gikuyu would dream of marrying a girl who has not been circumcised and vice versa*

Kenyatta, 1953

Whilst these words were spoken in 1953, more recent findings of a survey closer to home which looked at the experiences, attitudes and beliefs of single Somali men living in London, revealed that over a third of those questioned said they would want to marry a circumcised woman, and just under half of those surveyed maintained that they would circumcise their daughters and not be deterred by the law (Williams, 1998).

Many, both in the UK and elsewhere, strongly believe that to deviate from this tradition will have far reaching consequences on their communities and lead to a breakdown in society. These arguments from a *cultural self-determination* stance are difficult to challenge, and westerners especially, who condemn the practice and lobby for its eradication, are often accused of imposing their western norms on other cultures, as the following quote summarises:

> *The overwhelming majority believe that the secret aim of those who attack this centuries old custom is to disintegrate their social order and thereby hasten their Europeanisation*

Kenyatta, 1953

Is this a valid argument warranting serious consideration? After all, are there not equivalent unhealthy and dangerous practices carried out in western societies, which, arguably, can have far reaching negative consequences on the health and well-being of individuals? Arguably, there are blatant double standards around these issues, and advocators of FC point to cosmetic surgical operations, voluntary participation, consent and the superiority-inferiority debate as evidence. These will now be explored a little further.

The 'cosmetic surgery' debate

Let us consider sex change operations or cosmetic surgical operations such as breast enlargement/reduction, face-lifts, operations to remove ribs in order to achieve a slimmer form – which are all carried out in the name of beauty. Might these practices be regarded upon by some – and particularly those in non-white cultures, as immoral, barbaric and potentially damaging physically or psychologically? Certainly, many proponents of FGM see these as unnecessary and contravening the various UN human rights conventions.

Voluntary participation and consent

With cosmetic surgery such as breast enlargement/reduction, face-lifts, etc., it is normally individuals over the age of consent that make the decision to undergo such procedures. In most cases of FGM, however, it is parents or adult family members who take the ultimate decision to have their daughters circumcised, and girls are not necessarily informed beforehand.

The anomaly, however, is in cases where individuals wish to assert their right to FGM during adulthood and, in particular, following childbirth where they may request re-infibulation. Whilst the latter is carried out by practitioners at the request of women in some countries around the world (including the USA), in others, such as the UK, it is outlawed on the grounds that consent to serious injury should not be legitimised and practitioners can be prosecuted for carrying out such requests by women. This, again, is often perceived as double standards and racist.

Whose right is it anyway? The superiority-inferiority debate

Who then has the right to decide what constitutes acceptable or unacceptable behaviour? Many black and minority ethnic people in the UK and elsewhere, feel that the concept of the practice as 'genital mutilation' is a western phenomenon, and an attempt by the West to impose its views upon other cultures and societies. But what gives the West superiority over other nations and cultures to determine what is acceptable and unacceptable? This brings in the 'race' debate around cultural superiority-inferiority whereby economically and politically powerful cultures justify *their* evil, barbaric, and cruel practices as acceptable and right, and dismiss cultures inferior to them, branding their practices primitive, backward, and in the case of FGM, illegal and immoral (Shweder, 2000). This can be explained in relation to abortion, which *has* been and continues to be a religious and human rights issue, in violation of the rights of the unborn child. However, because of the ever increasing teenage pregnancy rate and a culture of promiscuity, the West has had to redefine its boundaries of human rights by excluding abortion. Abortion has become a normal part of everyday life and culture, such that opposition to it is regarded as deplorable. In comparison, how then does female circumcision become a human rights issue?

Over the years, whilst cultures and nations have found a lot of common ground, they have also struggled to find codes of conduct, which could be meaningfully applied to all. The difficulty lies in the diverse mix of cultures within and between nations, such that what is deemed acceptable in one society may be regarded as unacceptable by another or by the same people in a different time period in history. The latter is indeed true of FGM, which, as discussed in detail in chapter six, was practised widely and accepted in one form or another by nations which now abhor it.

CHAPTER THREE

FEMALE CIRCUMCISION IN ISLAM

Introduction

Over the years the practice of FGM has increasingly come to be linked to religious obligatory practices and, particularly, to Islam. El-Dareer (1983b) points out that this is evident from various attitudinal surveys that have investigated why people insist upon the practice. Modesty and chastity are used to justify the practice by many who carry it out, as well as by some religious leaders. The popular assumption that FGM is an Islamic practice may be due to the fact that the pharaonic type circumcision, which is the severest form, is mainly practised by countries where Islam is the principal religion. It is, therefore, important to explore what Islam says about FGM, where the Islamic Sharia (divine law) stands on this issue, and what are the views of leading Islamic ulemas. This is critical for three reasons: to help our understanding of its religious significance, to be able to work effectively with those who may agree or insist on the practice because of its religious obligation and to help those who may wish to devise policies or strategies sensitive to religious beliefs.

The Muslim context in the West

Post World War II western societies have witnessed significant changes to their population trends. More and more have become multi-cultural, multi-racial and multi-faith. Muslims are now an integral part of most multi-faith western societies. According to census statistics and population estimates there are 23 million in Europe (Vertoved and Peach, 1997) and between six and eight million in the USA (Ali, 1996). In some countries like Britain, Muslims are the largest religious minority group with a population of well over 1.5 million, and almost 60 per cent of them British born (ONS, 2003).

Muslims in the West, like the followers of Islam in other parts of the world, are extremely diverse. They come from different countries, and belong to different ethnic groups and racial origins. Even though the core Islamic values, provided by the teachings of the Qur'an and Sunna are common amidst all this diversity, ethnic and cultural values are *not* common nor are Muslims of different ethnic groups necessarily aware of each other's cultures, traditions and practices. An African Muslim, for example, will not necessarily be aware of the cultures and traditions of a Pakistani Muslim and vice versa.

Consequently, most Muslims of non-African backgrounds have never heard of issues like FGM that are practised and justified by certain other Muslim communities. Whilst appreciating the rights to cultural differences and the rights to defend traditional values and practices, many feel a clear sense of shock and horror that FGM can be held to be an Islamic religious requirement. Their response is clear and simple: this is a cultural not an Islamic practice. FGM is a crime in Islam. The culture or custom of FGM did not originate from Islam nor do all Muslims, as in the examples of Saudi Arabia, Iraq, Iran, Algeria, Morocco, Tunisia, Libya, and Pakistan, follow it. As one leading British Muslim Scholar, Maulana Qamaruzzaman Azmi, Secretary General of the World Islamic Mission, points out:

> *Certain Muslim ethnic groups in West Africa and elsewhere tattoo their faces with scars by carving symbolic designs into their flesh. This is, however, a local custom rather than Islamic practice. It is not condoned by Islam*
>
> Azmi, 2003

It is, however, this rich ethnic diversity as well as the lack of a national Muslim forum in the UK and in the West, that has not allowed for a coherent programme of action against FGM by Muslims. In most countries where Islam is the principal religion, measures have been taken to stamp out the practice (see chapter five). Whilst there is a network of about 1000 Mosques in the UK alone to provide a strong platform for action, the issue of FGM is not relevant for 99.9 per cent of them. This is because the number of Muslims who practise FGM are from certain parts of Africa and are therefore extremely small in number. In Britain for example, the largest number of Muslims originate from Pakistan (about 700,000) with sizeable groups from Bangladesh, India, Cyprus, Malaysia, and the Arab countries. There is only a small population from Europe and Africa along with an increasing number of white English Muslims, about 10,000, who are mostly converts to Islam (Anwar and Bakhsh, 2003).

Whilst many Imams and scholars in the UK need to be informed about this practice, some who are aware have taken it upon themselves to help in the campaign for eradication and elimination (see chapter six for further details).

The place of female genital mutilation in Islam

The Arabic word for circumcision is derived from the verb 'khatana', which means to cut or sever, and the word 'khitan' is used for both the procedure of circumcision and for the part of the body which is circumcised. Male circumcision, although predating Islam, is a Muslim tradition. Although it is not prescribed in the Qur'an, it was approved by the Holy Prophet (pbuh), and he himself was circumcised. The practice of FC also predates Islam. It is not mentioned in the Qur'an nor is it approved by Islam. Nevertheless, proponents and practitioners have tended to use religion and religious values of modesty, chastity and purity to justify the practice. The practice of FC is, however, not exclusive to Islam but found amongst all religious groups living in certain parts of Africa where longstanding local cultural traditions have been linked with religious beliefs.

Tradition carries its own validity and the status quo is never questioned. The fact that the practice of FGM is deep rooted in countries where illiteracy and poverty are widespread and the source of education are familial or cultural sayings and traditions passed down, is clearly a key factor in the maintenance of the practice. This also explains why women are the strongest proponents of the practice. They grow up within the context of their cultural norms accepting physical and psychological suffering, knowing that in any other state they will be seen as unacceptable, socially ostracised and will not be sought out for marriage.

Islamic legal rulings are deduced from the original universally agreed sources. These are the Qur'an, the authentic Sunna (practices) of the Prophet (pbuh), consensus (subject to the conditions set for it in the principles of Islamic jurisprudence), and analogy (when it meets the essential conditions). The Qur'an makes no mention, either explicit or implicit, of female circumcision. There is no consensus on the ruling of Islamic law with regard to it, and no analogy that it is relevant and admissible.

The Sunna is the only source to which the presumed legitimacy is extracted. This is because of certain quotations attributed to the Prophet (pbuh) in some anthologies of hadith. Dr Muhammad Salim al-Awwa, a leading Egyptian Islamic scholar, however, points out that there is no authentic evidence in the hadith for sanctioning such an act. Islamic Scholars do not admit the evidence of any hadith which has questionable authority. Evidence can be taken only from those that have a strong chain of source and transmission. However, the hadith most often quoted to support the act of female circumcision is one that concerns a woman called Umm Attia, said to have practised female circumcision in Medina. It is claimed that the Prophet (pbuh) told her:

> *Umm Attia, do not cut severely as that is more pleasant for a woman and more preferable for a husband*
> Abu Dawood's Sunan, 1354 AH

This hadith is quoted, with similar phraseology, by Al-Hakim, Al-Baihaqi, and Abu Dawood. All of them, however, relate it with weak chains of transmission, as hadith scholar Zein al-Din al-Iraqi points out in his commentary on Al-Ghazali's Ihya-ulum al-din (1:148). Abu Dawood points out that this hadith is reported in its general sense on the authority of Ubaidullah ibn Amr ibn Abdal Malik.

> *Its chain of transmitters is not strong. Besides, it is reported not as a direct quote attributed to the Prophet (pbuh)...This hadith is poor in authenticity*
> Abu Dawood's Sunnas, 1354 AH

Dr Muhammad Lutfi al-Sabbagh, an authoritative Islamic Scholar in Saudi Arabia, and Professor of Islamic Studies at King Saud University, Riyadh, states that:

> *Abu Dawood mentions the hadith only to point out its weakness. There is, therefore, no authentic report nor sunna to be followed in regards to female circumcision...it is unlikely that the Holy Prophet (pbuh) would address a woman (Umm Attia), and be so candid with her, on such a subject, using the words, 'that is more pleasant for the woman and more preferable to her husband'*
> Al-Sabbagh, 1996

Dr Muhammad Lutfi al-Sabbagh goes on to state in his article that:

> *even if the hadith is authentic, it does not imply that circumcision is a 'requirement'. All it does is to forbid removing too much of the parts concerned*
> Al-Sabbagh, 1996

Thus, Umm Attia's hadith, in all its versions, has been dismissed by the world's Islamic scholars from all four schools of fiqh (thought) – Shafie, Hanafi, Hanbali, and Malkie – as of no value and unable to serve as evidence.

Another hadith, which is as well known, is that involving Umm Attia in a quotation attributed to the Prophet (pbuh), which says:

circumcision is a Sunna for men and a sign of respect for women.

In his comments on Ihya ulum al-din, hadith scholar al-Iraqi finds it also lacking in authenticity. For this and other reasons, the most eminent scholar Sheikh Sayyed Sabeq says in Fiqh al-Sunna that:

the hadiths recommending female circumcision are poor in authenticity. None of them is found to be authentic.

In his book 'Talkhis al-habir fi takhrij ahadith al-rafie al-kabiri', hadith scholar Ibn Hajar describes this hadith as poor in authenticity, and quotes Imam al-Baihaqi's point of view that it is:

poor, with a broken chain of transmissions

Al-Baihaqi, 1066AH

In al-tamhid lima fil-muwatta' min al-ma'ani wal-assanid, hadith scholar Abu Umar Ibn Abd al-Barr says:

it is based on the authority of a transmitter whose report cannot be admitted as evidence.

Abu Dawood, 1354

Abu Umar Ibn Abd al-Barr goes further in his book to say that:

those who consider (female) circumcision a sunna, use as evidence this hadith of Abu al-Malih, which is based solely on the evidence of Hajjaj Ibn Artaa, who cannot be admitted as an authority when he is the sole transmitter. The consensus of Muslim scholars shows that circumcision is for men

Abu Dawood, 1354

Muslim scholars, therefore, are unanimous that the two hadith are weak and cannot be accepted as evidence. Dr Muhammad Salim al-Awwa states that:

had the Prophet intended an equal ruling for men and women, he would have said: 'circumcision is a sunna for men and women', or he might have said: 'circumcision is a sunna', and stopped at that. That would have made the ruling general, as long as it does not have anything which restricts its application to some, and not to all people

Al-Awwa, 1994

There is, however, an authentic hadith in which Aisha, wife of the Prophet (pbuh), directly quotes the Prophet (and with a version where she is the one quoted) as saying something, cited in more than one version with slightly different phraseology, to the effect that:

if the two circumcision organs meet, ghusl or ablution, becomes
obligatory

Al-Tirmithi, 1343 AH

This hadith is cited by Imam Malik in Al-Muwatta, Imam Muslim in his anthology of authentic hadith, Al-Tirmithi and Ibn Majah in their anthologies, and other editors of collections of the hadith. However, the relevant point here is the phrase 'two circumcision organs' used by the Prophet which is an explicit reference to male and female organs that are usually circumcised and which is taken by some people as evidence that clitoridectomy is legitimate.

Muslim scholars, however, point out that this authentic hadith is by no means evidence of legitimacy. The Arabic word used for 'the two circumcision organs' is in the dual case and it follows the habit of calling two objects or two persons after the one more familiar or after either of them, giving it prominence. There are many examples of this in idiomatic Arabic usage, such as 'the two Umars', referring to Abu Bakr and Umar; 'the two moons', referring to the sun and moon; 'the shining two', making the same reference although the moon does not shine of itself and only reflects the light of the sun. Arabs usually choose the more prominent of the two or the easier in giving a dual form, and that is why they say for parents, 'the two fathers', although they are a father and a mother. This usage in the Arabic language is familiar to Arabic linguists. Thus, Al-Awwa (1994) points out that:

> *in true Sunna there is no evidence that female circumcision is*
> *endorsed, that all the hadith on female circumcision used as*
> *evidence are poor on authenticity and can not serve as the basis*
> *for a religious ruling, and that the practice is nothing other than*
> *a custom which Islam left for time and for progress in medicine*
> *to refine or abolish.*

Islamic scholars state that Islam does not suppress women's sexuality, nor considers sex as something shameful and, therefore, to deny a woman's legitimate right to enjoy intimacy with her husband is a flagrant assault on that person (Al-Awwa, 1994). The female genitals in their normal form and as created by God are not a disease, nor a cause of disease. Nor do they cause any sort of pain, which requires surgical intervention. Thus, any surgical tampering with this delicate, natural system, in any of the forms of female circumcision, is not regarded by the law as falling under any of the valid reasons for surgery – which are medical treatment, detection of a disease, relief from a current pain or prevention of an expected one. Therefore, female circumcision is not allowed and calls for punishment (Al-Awwa, 1994). Dawood (1996) a leading Sudanese Islamic Scholar sates:

> *a man who allows his daughter to be subjected to circumcision...is damned in Islamic law. He commits a major and cardinal sin. The same is true of any mother or woman who performs it*
>
> Dawood, 1996

Thus it is clear that clitoridectomy cannot be legitimate under Islamic law, particularly since nothing that recommends it is definitely established as said by the Prophet. It is, therefore, neither an obligation nor a Sunna. Nor is it a sign of respect because all the hadith endorsing it are poor in authenticity. It is rather a custom and as such is not common in all Islamic countries. What is, however, established is the hadith of the Prophet in which he says:

> *Do not harm yourself or others*
>
> Al-Tirmithi, 1343 AH

This hadith is one of the basic principles of Islam. Therefore, Al-Sabbagh (1996) states that:

> *the view taken by a great number of scholars in the absence of any hadith that may be authentically attributed to the Prophet is that female circumcision is a major crime in Islamic law.*

CHAPTER FOUR

INTERNATIONAL INFORMATION
CONVENTIONS, FRAMEWORKS AND INITIATIVES
IN WESTERN COUNTRIES

Introduction

This chapter surveys the international scene and acts as a reference point on the issue of female circumcision globally. It explores the various international conventions and declarations protecting the rights of women and calling for appropriate and effective measures by individual states to eradicate female circumcision. It also looks at the role of key international organisations, actions within other international forums as well as the western response to FGM by highlighting the situation in Australia, Canada, the United States and Europe. Action within the UK is discussed in chapter six.

The worldwide context

Worldwide prevalence of FGM is estimated to be about 140 million, with an additional two million girls and women undergoing the procedure every year. The practice is prevalent in more than 26 African countries and among a few minority groups in parts of Asia and Arabia. The prevalence in African countries varies widely from about 5 per cent in the Democratic Republic of Congo (former Zaire) and Uganda to 98 per cent in Somalia. In addition, there are many immigrant women in Europe, Canada, and the United States who have undergone FGM. It is estimated that 15 per cent of all circumcised women have undergone the most severe infibulation-type.

FGM was not addressed purposefully on an international level until the late 1970s. Previous attempts to introduce the issue to the agendas of international organisations were unsuccessful due to a reluctance in getting involved and being seen to be interfering with an issue so bound up in social and cultural norms. In the 1970s, however, this changed when individuals began speaking out on the issue, and documents and articles began to appear in various journals and magazines in Africa and elsewhere. These included *The silence over FGM in Kenya*, (1978, Viva Magazine), articles on cases of FGM in the Sudanese family planning magazine *Happy Family*, and the 1978 publication of *La Parole aux Negresses*, by Awa Thiam, a young Senegalese woman. July 1978 saw the publication of Fran Hosken's research findings the *Epidemiology of FGM* published in Tropical Doctor.

As a result of public interest in the issue, moves were made to address it at an international level, and today, many African countries have illegalised the practice and are working closely with communities to change attitudes and practices. Whilst many international organisations have signed up to supporting the cause against FGM, there is still no lead organisation co-ordinating all the work going on in the area, and the onus is still left to individual countries and their citizens.

In this chapter, we will first explore the various international conventions and declarations ratified and adopted by most FGM-practising countries. We will then look at the role of some of the key international organisations and give an outline of initiatives that have been adopted by some FGM-practising countries, to promote the reduction and elimination of FGM and to enhance the social wellbeing of women.

International Conventions and Declarations

Most FGM-practising countries have ratified international conventions and declarations that make provisions for the promotion and protection of the health of girls and women. These include:

1948: The Universal Declaration of Human Rights
  - Article 25 proclaims the right of all human beings to live in conditions that allow them to enjoy good health and health care.

1966: The International Covenants on Civil and Political Rights and on Economic, Social and Cultural Rights
  - Article 12 (as quoted previously in chapter two).

1979: The Convention on the Elimination of All Forms of Discrimination against Women (CEDAW)
  - Article 2f requires State Parties to take measures against all customs and practices which constitute discrimination against women.

- Article 5 (as quoted previously in chapter two).
- *General Recommendation 24 to the Article 12 of the Convention* (on women and health) recommends the need for State Parties to ensure the enactment and effective enforcement of laws that prohibit FGM which carry a high risk of death and disability.
- *General Recommendation 14 (1990) relates particularly to FGM.* It recommends that State Parties take appropriate and effective measures to eradicate female circumcision; to collect and disseminate basic data on traditional practices; to support women's organisations at local and national levels that work towards the elimination of harmful practices; to encourage politicians, professionals, religious and community leaders to co-operate in influencing attitudes; to introduce appropriate educational and training programmes; to include appropriate strategies aimed at eradication of female circumcision into national health policies; to invite assistance, information and advice from the appropriate organisation of the United Nations; and to include in their reports to the Committee under Articles 10 and 12 of the Convention information about measures taken to eliminate female circumcision.

1990: The Convention on the Rights of the Child

- Article 19.1 protects against all forms of mental and physical violence and maltreatment.
- Article 37a provides freedom from torture or cruel, inhuman or degrading treatment.
- Article 24.3 requires State Parties to take all effective and appropriate measures to abolish traditional practices prejudicial to the health of children.

The African Charter on the Welfare of the Child

- Article 21 requires State Parties to take all appropriate measures to eliminate harmful social and cultural practices affecting the welfare, dignity, normal growth and development of the child and specifically defines protection against customs and practices prejudicial to the health or life of the child; and customs and practices discriminatory to the child on the grounds of sex or other status.

1993: The Vienna Declaration and the Programme of Action of the World Conference on Human Rights

- This expanded the international human rights agenda to include gender-based violence including FGM.

1994: The Programme of Action of the International Conference on Population and Development

1995: The Platform for Action of the Fourth World Conference on Women
- This urged the governments, international organisations and NGOs to develop policies and programmes to eliminate all forms of discrimination against the girl child, including FGM.

1997: The African Charter on Human and Peoples' Rights
- Article 4 on integrity of person.
- Article 5 on human dignity and protection against degradation.
- Article 16 on the right to health.
- Article 18 (3) on protection of the rights of women and children.

The Addis Ababa Declaration
- The Organisation of African Unity (OAU) adopted the Addis Ababa Declaration on violence against women. This declaration was later endorsed by the Assembly of Heads of State and governments and marked an important step towards the development of an African Charter on violence against women, providing the framework for national laws against FGM.

1998: The Banjul Declaration
- The Inter-African Committee on Traditional Practices Affecting the Health of Women and Children in collaboration with the Gambian Committee on Traditional Practices. (GAMCOTRAP) organised a symposium for religious leaders and medical personnel in Banjul, Gambia on 20 July 1998. The Symposium issued a communiqué, a declaration and recommendations condemning and demanding the eradication of FGM and other harmful practices.

1999: The United Nations Social, Humanitarian and Cultural Committee (Third Committee)
- This Committee approved a resolution that calls upon States to implement legislation and policies that prohibit traditional or customary practices affecting the health of women and girls including FGM.

The Ouagadougou Declaration
- This Workshop of the West African Economic and Monetary Union (UEMOA) held in Ouagadougou on 4 May 1999 made three recommendations: to prepare an African Charter on FGM; to adopt specific legislation against FGM in all UEMOA States (West African Economic and Monetary Union); and to establish sub-regional networks of traditional and religious leaders, and modern and traditional communicators, to support national committees in their campaign against FGM.

Key Actions for Further Implementation of the Programme of Action of the International Conference on Population and Development
- This called for governments to promote human rights of women and girls and freedom from coercion, discrimination, violence including harmful practice, and sexual exploitation and to review national legislation and amend those that discriminate against girls and women.

2000 *Further Actions and Initiatives to Implement the Beijing Declaration and Platform for Action*
- This recognises the progress made by governments in implementing legislation to ban FGM. However, it called for governments to take action to combat and eliminate violence against women that is incompatible with the dignity and worth of the person.

The role of key international organisations

The World Health Organisation (WHO)
In the late 1950s, efforts by the Economic and Social Council (ECOSOC) of the United Nations (UN) to engage the World Health Organisation (WHO) in a study to investigate customs around the world that subject girls to ritual operations, met with much resistance from the WHO, on the grounds of the cultural and social complexities. It was not until February 1979 at a WHO seminar organised in Khartoum that the first opportunity arose for discussing the issue of FGM. The seminar brought together representatives from Sudan, Oman, Somalia, Djibouti, Kenya, Nigeria, Egypt, Burkina Faso, Ethiopia and South Yemen, who met to discuss 'Traditional Practices Affecting the Health of Women and Children.' A number of recommendations aimed at individual governments were proposed as a result of the seminar,

which included the need for governments to introduce clear national policies in the move to abolish FGM, to establish national co-ordinating commissions to oversee all activities on the issue, and to increase education at a community and professional level – emphasising the dangers of FGM. In the absence of an international monitoring body to oversee the implementation of these recommendations across individual countries, it is not known how much these recommendations were implemented. What is known is that the action taken by different countries was variable. In 1989, the Regional Committee of the WHO for Africa passed a resolution urging participating governments:

> to adopt appropriate policies and strategies in order to abolish female circumcision and to forbid medicalisation of female circumcision and to discourage health professionals from performing such surgery

> WHO, Resolution of the Regional Committee for Africa,
> 39th session, 13 September, 1989

United Nations Education Scientific and Cultural Organisation (UNESCO)

Whilst many conferences, debates and research studies have been organised around cultural practices in Africa, surprisingly UNESCO has had very little dealings with the issue of FGM from the point of view of data collection or educational campaigns. In 1980, the human rights division of UNESCO did begin to sponsor research programmes into FGM.

United Nations (UN)

The decade 1975-1985 was declared the UN's decade for women. In 1980, a major UN conference was held in Copenhagen to review progress to date on a number of key themes including health, education, and employment. FGM was not brought up as an issue by any African country during the conference, though the Swedish delegates did raise it as an issue, pledging their support to any country concerned who were wanting to undertake activities to address the issue. The NGO forum which ran in parallel to the conference and had 8,000 women from 120 countries, adopted a more hands on approach, holding workshops, discussions, debates, slide shows, lectures, and press conferences on the issue. Whilst highly emotive, the session was felt to have enlightened many who had previously condemned the practice without taking account of the various social, cultural and economic considerations within which the practice is deeply embedded. The UN Convention on the Rights of the Child is ambiguous about FGM. On one hand, Article 24, paragraph 3 states:

> *State Parties shall take all effective and appropriate measures with a view to abolishing traditional practices prejudicial to the health of children.*

But Article 29 paragraph 1c calls for:

> *The development of respect for the child's parents, his or her own cultural identity, language and values, for the national values of the country in which the child is living, the country from which he or she may originate, and for civilisations different from his or her own.*

It was not until 1991 that the first seminar on Harmful Traditional Practices and Human Rights was organised by the UN Human Rights Commission, held in Ouagadougou, Burkina Faso.

United Nations Populations Fund (UNFPA)

Activities for the eradication of FGM are integrated into the core areas of the UNFPA mandate, which includes family planning and sexual health, population and development strategies, and advocacy. Support is given to parents, teachers and community leaders for various activities around FGM issues. There is also support for advocacy, policy and legal reforms, and the provision of reproductive and sexual health care. UNFPA also works in collaboration with national and regional NGOs that are advocating against and educating around the issue of FGM.

United Nations Children's Fund (UNICEF)

UNICEF first became active on the issue of FGM in March 1980, when it announced its anti-FGM programme as:

> *based on the belief that the best way to handle the problem is to trigger awareness through education of the public, members of the medical profession and practitioners of traditional health care with the help of local collectives and their leaders.*
>
> UNICEF, 1980

A joint plan of action was launched in conjunction with the WHO, outlining the need for research on the issue of FGM, dissemination of these findings, and identification of useful organisations. Whist outlining these recommendations, however, responsibility for their implementation was left to the appropriate authorities in individual countries rather than a centrally led body. A series of multi media communication campaigns had also been developed by UNICEF, focusing on harmful practices. Topics were raised through entertaining stories about fictional characters, using various methods including video, radio, comic and storybooks, toys, and other educational materials. UNICEF and the WHO also assisted with the setting up of the Inter-African Committee on Traditional Practices (IAC) which was established in 1984, has financed meetings, training workshops and information campaigns aimed at activists, community members, and health workers. In September 1997, it held a symposium for legislators at the headquarters of the Organisation of African Unity (OAU) in Ethiopia. At this symposium, the Addis Ababa Declaration was issued calling on African governments to take a clear policy-driven stance in the move to significantly reduce incidence of FGM by the year 2005. To date, of the 29 FGM-practising countries, 22 have branches of the IAC.

In 1997, a joint statement was issued by WHO, UNICEF, and UNFPA expressing commitment from all three organisations towards abolition of the practice. It also called for top down support to complement grass roots work, and noted that

> *whilst female genital mutilation continues as a deeply rooted traditional practice, culture is in constant flux and is capable of adapting and reforming*

World Health Organisation, 1997

Action within other international forums

Various other international NGOs have been involved with the work on FGM, including the Foundation for Women's Health, Research and Development (FORWARD), the Minority Rights Group (MRG), the Agency for Culture and Change Management (ACCM), the Research, Action and Information Network for the Bodily Integrity of Women (Rainbo), Equality Now, and Amnesty International. All have been instrumental not only in researching, supporting and sometimes setting up grassroots initiatives, but also in lobbying to push it forward on UK government and international agendas.

The African symposium on *The World of Work and the Protection of the Child* held in Cameroon in December 1979, recommended campaigning against excision through teaching and education. The second regional conference on *The Integrity of Women in Development* in Lusaka, held in 1979, unanimously adopted a resolution condemning infibulation, urging African governments to assist in the search for a solution to the problem. In 1982, the International Council of Nurses adopted a resolution against FGM, whilst the international seminar of the Commission Internationale pour l'Abolition des Mutilations Sexuelles (CAMS) held in Senegal in 1982 voted to establish a centre for research and education into the practice of FGM. In September 1982, the International Congress on Child Abuse and Neglect held three workshops on the issue of FGM. The IAC and CAMS organised a number of workshops within the NGO forum, at a conference held in Nairobi in July 1985 to mark the end of the United Nations Women's Decade. June 1988 saw an international seminar organised in Somalia by the Somali Women's Democratic Organisation and the Italian Association for Women in Development on *Female Circumcision: Strategies to Bring About Change.* CAMS-France hosted an international conference in Paris, looking at *Violence and Sexual Mutilation inflicted on Girls and Women.* In March 2001 a conference supported by UNICEF and United Nation's agencies for women (UNIFEM), was held in the Parisian Congress Palace in Paris. It was attended by representatives from several NGOs and UN agencies, all appealing for the total abolition of FGM.

Western responses to FGM

Several industrialised countries including Australia, Belgium, Canada, Denmark, New Zealand, Norway, Sweden, the United Kingdom and the United States, that receive immigrants from countries where FGM is practised, have outlawed it. In Australia, six of its eight states have passed laws against it, whilst in the United States, the federal government and 16 states have criminalised it. In addition to legislation, various countries have attempted to engage their FGM-practising communities in a dialogue about the issue. A number of positive initiatives to abolish the practice have been developed in some countries in conjunction with community groups, NGOs, and international organisations. What follows is a brief overview of the initiatives by some of these countries.

Australia

Prevalence rates and types of FGM carried out

According to the 1991 Australian Bureau of Statistics Census, there were approximately 76,000 immigrant females from FGM-practising countries living in Australia.

Action on eradication

From 1995-2000, the Australian government committed to a National Education Programme on FGM(NEPFGM), which aimed to discourage practice through community education, information and support.

Current legislation on FGM

Specific legislation banning FGM was introduced into six of Australia's eight states over the period 1994-1997. In Queensland and Western Australia, however, legislation against FGM relies on the criminal code in relation to assault. In the states where FGM is outlawed, penalties of up to seven years' imprisonment apply to persons convicted of intentionally performing FGM, or for taking or arranging for a child (under 18 years of age) out of a jurisdiction for the purpose of performing FGM. Exceptions are made in the case of medical procedures that have a 'genuine therapeutic purpose'.

Canada

Prevalence rates and types of FGM carried out

FGM affects girls and women of certain immigrant populations settled in Canada – many of whom are from Somalia.

Action on eradication

Abolition initiatives around FGM by Canada's federal government have been underway for several years. One major initiative in the mid 1990s was the setting up of a Federal Interdepartmental Ad Hoc Working Group on FGM, to discuss the most appropriate way in which to educate members of the FGM-practising communities on a number of issues around the practice. These included Canadian law, health risks, and cultural/religious issues. Consultations were carried out over two months in both Ottawa and Montreal with members of communities in which FGM is a traditional practice, which led to the publication of the Ontario FGM Prevention Task Force Report, providing concrete recommendations. Some of the recommendations made included the need to provide information to communities about legal implications and health risks associated with FGM in a culturally sensitive and appropriate manner, and for various members of the community – including health professionals, religious leaders, and community leaders, to be actively involved in the delivery of information. The need to avoid offensive terminology and discourage media sensationalism was also one of the recommendations made.

Current legislation on FGM

FGM has been specifically outlawed in Canada since 1997. Those found in breach of the law are liable to imprisonment for a term of up to fourteen years. It is also unlawful for girls resident in Canada to be taken out of the country and circumcised abroad, for which the penalty is up to five years' imprisonment.

New Zealand

Prevalence rates and types of FGM carried out
FGM in New Zealand affects women and girls of certain immigrant populations including Sudanese, Somali, and Ethiopian.

Action on eradication
New Zealand has actively supported international efforts to eliminate FGM as well as other traditional practices which affect the health of women and girls. It co-sponsored the biennial resolution on *Traditional or Customary Practices Affecting the Health of Women and Girls* at the third committee of the UN General Assembly, as well as the resolution on the *Elimination of Violence Against Women* at the Commission on Human Rights. Furthermore, New Zealand has ratified the Convention to Eliminate All Forms of Discrimination Against Women and the UN Convention on the Rights of the Child. More recently, the government has been concerned about the issue because of a continued increase of immigrants from the countries where FGM is the norm e.g. Sudan, Somalia, and Ethiopia.A national FGM awareness campaign was carried out amongst the African refugee communities in 1998 and 1999, during which workshops were organised, and educational materials distributed.

Current legislation on FGM
In February 2002, FGM was specified as unlawful in an amendment to the Crimes Act of 1961. For those individuals involved in performing or causing FGM to be performed, it is punishable by imprisonment of up to seven years. The amendment also covers girls who are citizens or ordinarily resident in New Zealand who are taken abroad to be circumcised, for which the same penalty applies to those arranging for this to be carried out.

Norway

FGM in Norway affects women and girls from various immigrant populations arriving from the countries that practice it.

Action on eradication
In October 2000, the Norwegian Parliament asked the government to formulate a plan of action on the eradication of FGM, with the aim of ensuring a co-ordinated approach by organisations and individuals. The resulting *Governmental Action Plan Against FGM* was prepared and issued by the Ministry of Children and Family Affairs and included raising awareness on information and legislation, a preventive outline of work

within the health service and schools, and the strengthening of ties with international organisations working on the issue. A National Resource Group was established to take this action plan forward and a project co-ordinator appointed to implement, co-ordinate and monitor it.

Current legislation on FGM

Whilst FGM was outlawed under the provision of the General Civil Penal Code, an additional Act was added in December 1995 to clarify various disputed areas. Those breaking the law face fines and imprisonment of up to eight years, depending on the severity of the procedure, and the consequences for the individual. The Act also covers Norwegian nationals and those resident there who are taken abroad to be circumcised.

Sweden

Prevalence rates and types of FGM carried out

FGM affects approximately 16,000 women and girls of certain immigrant population settled in Sweden, the majority of whom are of Somali, Sudanese or Ethiopian ethnic origin. This figure is believed to be an underestimate due to the unknown numbers of asylum seekers awaiting asylum permits.

Action on eradication

Sweden claims to be at the forefront in the European fight against FGM since the 1980s. In 1982, it adopted the *Act against Female Mutilation*, which also extended to prosecuting parents taking their daughter's abroad to be circumcised. In the early 1990s, a number of individuals from the communities practising FGM expressed an interest in working collaboratively in the campaign against the practice. This led to a decade of programmes devoted to tackling the issue and the establishment of RISK, an independent organisation working towards achieving the aims of the UN Convention on the Rights of the Child. RISK has also been involved in collecting prevalence data on FGM, building links with international organisations and working with communities to discuss methods of engaging them in discussions about the practice. Such efforts are believed to have gone some way to reducing the incidence of FGM in Sweden.

Current legislation on FGM

FGM has been outlawed in Sweden since 1982 and amendments to the Act have since been made on two occasions. Individuals in breach of the law, face imprisonment of between four to ten years, depending on the consequences to the victim. The law also covers those individuals of Swedish nationality or resident in Sweden who are taken abroad to be circumcised. To date, there has been one prosecution in Sweden.

United States of America

Prevalence rates and types of FGM carried out

FGM affects a number of immigrant populations settled in the USA from countries including Egypt, Ethiopia, Ghana, Kenya, Liberia, Nigeria, Uganda, United Republic of Tanzania, Sierra Leone, Somalia and Sudan. The overall population of these groups have increased three-fold in the last thirty years. According to the 1990 Census data, the number of females from FGM-practising communities was estimated to be 168,000.

Action on eradication

In accordance with the law, the Secretary of Health and Human Services is required to carry out a number of tasks. These include compiling a database of the number of circumcised individuals living in the USA, obtaining a profile of age and ethnicity with the aim of building collaborative links with representatives from these ethnic groups, and designing and implementing outreach activities to educate about the harmful effects of FGM.

Current legislation on FGM

The Federal law prohibiting FGM in the USA came into effect in 1997 stipulating that FGM carried out on those under the age of eighteen for reasons other than those specified in the Act was an offence punishable by fine and/or imprisonment of up to five years. Federal law, however, does not cover girls being taken abroad for circumcision. In addition, FGM legislation does not apply to women over the age of eighteen having the same consenting rights as those requesting cosmetic surgical procedures. Since 1998, however, ten states have outlawed the practice and the legislative framework differs from state to state. In some states FGM is outlawed irrespective of age. In others, there are no specific FGM-related laws but the practice is covered under child abuse laws.

The general European scene

Prevalence rates and types of FGM carried out

A study carried out in 1998 on the number of immigrants coming to Europe, indicated the number from FGM-practising countries to be highest in Britain, followed by France, Italy and Germany (see also chapter six). However, specific laws outlawing the practice exist only in three European countries: Sweden (1982), Norway (1998), and the United Kingdom (1985). In the rest of Europe, there are only general laws without specific reference to FGM.

Action on eradication

In 1998, the International Centre for Reproductive Health (ICRH) carried out a study of FGM in Europe. The European Network for the Prevention of FGM in Europe was subsequently founded in 1999, out of the recommendations that came out of this study. The overall aim of the network was to provide guidelines in a number of areas for European countries to adopt. The network had representation from eleven countries including the UK, and comprised four working groups: Health Care Sector, NGOs, Community Based Organisations (CBOs), and the academic level – each with specific objectives. The aims of the Health Care Sector, for example, was to develop a framework for training health care professionals and to manage women who have been circumcised. The aims of the NGOs and CBOs were to exchange information and models of good practice at the grassroots level, whilst the aim of the academic unit was to set up a research facility and programme.

In November 2000, a hearing took place at the European Parliament to address the Europe-wide issue of FGM. A motion for a resolution to denounce FGM was tabled at the hearing inviting the Council, the Commission, and the member states to treat FGM as a crime against personal integrity, establish the prevalence of the practice within member states, promote information and prevention measures, recognise the risk of FGM as grounds for providing asylum or humanitarian protection, prioritise the fight against FGM as a priority human rights issue, and support NGOs working for the elimination of the practice in countries where it is justified by cultural and/or religious motivations.

In September 2001, the resolution on FGM was adopted by the European Parliament and called on the member states of the European Union to pursue, protect and punish any resident who had committed the crime of FGM, even if outside the frontier – 'extraterritoriality.' It also called on the Commission and the Council to take measures to protect victims of the practice, including recognising the right to asylum for women and girls at risk of FGM.

CHAPTER FIVE

INTERNATIONAL INFORMATION
PROGRAMMES AND STRATEGIES
IN AFRICAN COUNTRIES

Introduction

This chapter is intended to be a reference point for programmes and initiatives being undertaken by the majority of FGM-practising countries. Whilst efforts to implement international conventions and domestic legislation have been slow, this does not mean that nothing is happening. Several governments in Africa have taken steps to eliminate the practice of FGM in their countries. These range from laws criminalising the practice, to education and outreach programmes targeted at local communities, professionals, and community leaders. There have, however, been very few instances of adjudicated cases, since the enforcement of laws regarding FGM has on the whole been extremely lax or non-existent. Furthermore, the cultural norms in these countries or regions often render women unwilling to discuss FGM, let alone seek protection or compensation under the law.

Northeast Africa

Djibouti

Prevalence rates and types of FGM carried out
The two forms of FGM widely practised throughout Djibouti are excision (Type II) and infibulation (Type III), the latter being the most common form. Various estimates have indicated 90 to 98 per cent of young girls in Djibouti as having undergone one or other form of circumcision, which is usually carried out between the ages of five and ten.

Action on eradication
In 1987, a National Committee comprising members from the Ministries of Health, Justice and Education, the Red Crescent Society and the Union Nationale des Femmes de Djibouti (UNFD), was set up under the umbrella of UNFD to advocate for the abolition of FGM. One

initiative by UNFD was the setting up of a dispensary at its headquarters where girls were brought in for excision-type operations to be carried out by a traditional excisor under local anaesthetic. It was believed that this 'less radical' form of circumcision could be encouraged through such an approach thus protecting girls from infibulation. In a number of cases, however, grandmothers complained that the procedure was incomplete, and made arrangements to then have the girls infibulated. UNFD consequently closed its dispensary.

The government has since incorporated FGM awareness into its national programme promoting safe motherhood. A designated individual was appointed at the Ministry of Health to deal specifically with women's health issues. NGOs and other international organisations have the freedom to disseminate information and provide training and education about the harmful effects of the practice. The Ministry of Health has also allowed clinics and health training centres to be used for distributing information about FGM and other harmful health practices. It also works closely with various NGOs, UNICEF, and other organisations. Neighbourhood leaders have been appointed to promote public awareness campaigns, and the media has also been encouraged by the Ministry of Information to cover conferences on the topic.

In 1997, the National Committee of the Inter-African Committee on Traditional Practices Affecting the Health of Women and Children (IAC) in Djibouti produced a film on FGM and other harmful traditional practices, which was shown on national television. After the showing a roundtable discussion was held with members of IAC/Djibouti, doctors, religious leaders, traditional healers and birth attendants. All agreed that the practice had harmful health consequences and was not justified by science, religion or culture.

UNICEF and the World Health Organisation (WHO) are the major international organisations involved in campaigns in Djibouti. Anecdotal evidence suggests an increased awareness of the harmful effects of this practice, and a move away from infibulation to excision-type circumcision. This has been attributed, in part, to increased public awareness through campaigns and openness among the population in discussing the subject, and media coverage through newspapers, TV and radio.

Since a major obstacle to disseminating information about this subject is the illiteracy rate, street theatre, story telling and other means of communication, more in line with the oral traditions of Djiboutian society, have been adopted to get the messages across.

Current legislation on FGM

FGM was outlawed in the country's revised Penal Code that went into effect in April 1995. Article 333 of the Penal Code states that persons found guilty of this practice will face a five-year prison term and a monetary fine. Enforcement, however, is not easy. UNFD is aware of only one case in which a young woman had to be hospitalised following an operation. The circumcisor, whilst advised not to continue her practice, had no formal charges brought against her.

Egypt

Prevalence rates and types of FGM carried out

Egypt is one of the only countries in the Middle East where FGM and more commonly clitoridectomy, is practised widely amongst Muslims and Coptic Christians across all ethnic groups. Excision and infibulation-type circumcision is also found amongst a few ethnic groups in the southern part of the country.

Preliminary analysis of the results of the Demographic and Health Surveys (DHS) conducted in Egypt in 2000, found that 97 per cent of women surveyed have undergone one of these procedures. The operation is more often carried out between the ages of seven and ten years.

Action on eradication

Discussion on the issue began in the 1950s between the Egyptian medical and NGO workers. A decree in 1959 by the Minister of Health banned medical practitioners from carrying out circumcision operations unless there were clear medical grounds for it. In practice, however, there was no effective way of policing this. In October 1979, a seminar was held in Cairo which brought together representatives from various bodies including the WHO, UNICEF, the Arab League, the Sudanese Embassy, and various NGOs and representatives from medical and research institutions. It was agreed that FGM was a mutilating and harmful practice having grave physical and psychological repercussions, and with no religious or scientific basis. On these grounds, participants concluded that it should be confronted and opposed. This led in 1982, to the appointment of a co-ordinator to oversee a three-year project funded by the Population Crisis Committee and the Cairo Family Planning Association, which included a programme of education and training for doctors, nurses, midwives, social workers and other professionals. 1985 saw the formation of a national committee to combat FGM, which targeted public education campaigns at mother child health clinics and family planning centres, as well as at secondary school students, young men, and female manual workers. Media links were also used to target the wider audience.

Stringent eradication efforts once again gained momentum in 1994, around the time of the International Conference on Population and Development in Cairo. Shortly after this, a United States Cable News Network showed an Egyptian girl undergoing circumcision by a local circumcisor in the absence of any anaesthetic. This sparked a public outcry in the West, and a national debate in Egypt. In an attempt to curb the traditional harmful methods of carrying out the operation, the Health Minister issued a decree in 1994 allowing physicians to carry out the procedure, under some circumstances, in a hospital or clinic setting. This move was harshly condemned internally and externally, and in 1997 a key court decision upheld the 1995 decree by the Minister of Health outlawing FGM carried out without a prescription from a senior gynaecologist.

UN and US aid have helped Egypt's health ministry to run extensive education campaigns pushing to get anti-FGM voices into the mainstream media. The Centre for Development and Population Activity (CEDPA) has also been active in its anti- FGM programmes, and encourages a 'Positive Deviance' approach, which emphasises the need for solutions to be found by communities themselves.

The Coptic Evangelical Organisation for Social Services (CEOSS) has also played an active role in discouraging the practice. In 1995, it initiated an anti-FGM programme targeting 7-13 year old girls at risk of FGM and then carrying out work with them and their families. Those involved in the programme advocated a number of factors as prerequisite to bringing about change. These included use of simple and positive information on abandoning FGM and the involvement and support of local leaders.

The senior Islamic authorities in Egypt, the Sheikh of Al-Azhar and the Mufti, have publicly stated on a number of occasions that this practice is not required in Islam and have also declared the practice to be a risk to health. The leader of the Egyptian Coptic community, Pope Shenouda, has also stated publicly that this practice is not required for religious reasons.

Current legislation on FGM

Moves to stop the practice of FGM began in 1959 when it was banned and punishable by fine and imprisonment. In the following decades, however, there have been changes to the legal stance adopted. At present, parliament has yet to consider passing a law specifically banning FGM. There are, however, provisions under the Penal Code involving 'wounding' and 'intentional infliction of harm leading to death', that might be applicable, in addition to a ministerial decree prohibiting the practice. Furthermore, the Court of Cassation (Egypt's highest appeals court) upheld a government banning of the practice in December 1997, prohibiting all medical and non-medical practitioners from performing FGM in either public or private facilities, except for medical reasons certified by the head of a hospital's obstetric department. Perpetrators risk the loss of their medical licence and can be subjected to criminal punishment, which under the Penal Code, includes charges of manslaughter in cases of death. There have been some press reports on the prosecution of at least thirteen individuals under this Penal Code, including doctors, midwives and barbers, accused of performing FGM that resulted in haemorrhage, shock and death.

Eritrea

Prevalence rates and types of FGM carried out

Clitoridectomy, excision and infibulation are the forms of FGM practised in Eritrea with one-third infibulation cases. It is practised amongst almost all religious and ethnic groups and, according to a 1997 demographic and health survey, 90 per cent of women are believed to have undergone one of these forms of circumcision, mostly when under the age of seven

Action on eradication

The Eritrean People's Liberation Front (EPLF), which led the fight for independence and formed the government in 1991, has worked since 1988 to abolish this practice. The government has actively supported anti-FGM work and, in 1996, the Ministry of Health issued its primary health care guidelines articulating government policy on the practice. This included consideration of the need to provide treatment, counselling and rehabilitation for women who suffer negative consequences as a result of FGM. It also pledged to discourage the practice by educating communities and groups that perform it.As such, in-service training to all primary health care workers has been carried out using training materials. In October 1996, the Health Ministry sponsored a safe motherhood workshop, where one of the themes was the negative health impact of FGM. Joint projects have also been carried out with the United Nations Children's Fund (UNICEF) and the

United Nations Population Fund (UNFPA) to design national and local level campaigns discouraging the practice. The government has also worked closely with youth and women's organisations as well as enlisting the leaders of Eritrea's largest religious groups in its campaign against the practice.

Current legislation on FGM

There is no specific law against FGM in Eritrea. The government decided not to outlaw the practice for fear of driving it underground.

Ethiopia

Prevalence rates and types of FGM carried out

All four types of FGM are practised in Ethiopia. The practice varies greatly according to ethnic group; Type I is practised amongst Amharas, Tigrayans and Jeberti Muslims living in Tigray, whilst Type II is found amongst the Gurages, Oromos, Shankilas, and some Tigrays. Type III is carried out in the areas bordering Sudan and Somalia, and found amongst the Afar, Somali, and Harari. Type IV is practised in the Amhara region by the Gojams. The age at which it is carried out also varies from seven days to sixteen years.

A 1985 UNICEF funded survey carried out by the Ministry of Health in five regions of Ethiopia revealed that about 90 per cent of all Ethiopian women had undergone some form of FGM. Today's estimates place the number of girls and women affected at nearly 30 million in Ethiopia.

Action on eradication

Some work has been done through the Ministry of Education, which ran an educational radio series broadcast telling of the harmful effects of FGM, with the same messages being repeated in women's meetings organised by the Democratic Women's Association of Tigray. The radio series, which began in 1995, is one of the many educational activities sponsored by the National Committee on Traditional Practices in Ethiopia – an organisation having a major impact on the lives of girls and women. Set up in 1987, the Committee comprises government officials, NGOs and UN agencies, including UNICEF. It runs sponsored workshops for trainers who work in communities, and sensitisation workshops for health professionals, clergy, traditional birth attendants, women and youth associations, the media and schools. By 1996, approximately 1,350 people had attended the sensitisation workshops, and 38,000 students had participated in school-based ones. Though no survey has been conducted to assess the progress in eliminating FGM and other harmful practices, informal feedback seems encouraging.

Current legislation on FGM

FGM is banned through Ethiopia's 1994 Constitution, which prohibits 'harmful traditional practices'. There is no additional specific legislation at present.

Sudan

The greatest concentration of infibulated women is found in Sudan and the Horn of Africa, where nearly all women are infibulated. These countries have also witnessed some of the most determined efforts to abolish the practice.

Prevalence rates and types of FGM carried out

According to a survey conducted from 1996 to 2000 by the Sudan National Committee on Traditional Practices (SNCTP) and Save the Children (Sweden), 87 per cent of urban women and 91 per cent of rural women of all ethnic and religious groups practice a form of FGM. Types I, II and III are practised in the northern part of the country, with the latter being the most prevalent. FGM, although not traditionally practised in the south, is becoming more prominent here due to the two million internally displaced southerners, living in the north today. In addition, there are a number of southern women who elect to undergo the procedure when marrying men from the north.

Action on eradication

Sudan has a long 50-year history of efforts to combat FGM, since Anglo-Egyptian times, but little has changed in terms of the numbers of infibulated women to date. Various organisations have been involved in the fight against it. The Organisation for Eradication of Traditional Harmful Practices Affecting the Health of Women and Children (ETHP) was established in 1984 by a resolution signed by the Minister of the Interior and Social Welfare. Its objective is to abolish the practice by focusing on instruction and information for key groups, through workshops, seminars, courses and discussions. The Mutawinat Group, established in 1990, held a workshop in 1997 that brought together governmental and NGOs. They pursued an innovative study documenting the status of women who had not undergone this procedure, and also worked to get information about the practice into school curricula. These, and other organisations, are recognised by the Ministry of the Interior and Social Welfare, which allows them to operate freely. They work closely with the United Nations Population Fund (UNFPA) under the Project for Information, Education and

Communication and the United Nations Children's Fund (UNICEF). Members of the medical profession are now involving themselves in the issue, which is starting to be discussed more openly. Eradication of Type III or infibulation was integrated into the curriculum for community health nurses at the Khartoum Nursing College. It is hoped this approach can also be included in the curriculum for medical students and student midwives.

With the weight of the present government behind it, an intensive campaign against the practice has been launched supported by religious groups, the media and women's organisations. Whist few have abandoned the practice of FGM altogether, many have opted for the milder sunna type.

Current legislation on FGM

Sudan is the first country in Africa to legislate against FGM. As early as 1930 an article urging for an end to the practice was written by a medical student, who outlined its harmful effects. In 1943, a medical committee was set up by the English Governor General to study the practice. This culminated in a media campaign condemning infibulation, on the grounds that it was cruel, harmful and associated with a whole array of negative repercussions. Since this was found to have been ineffective, the government in 1946 prohibited infibulation but permitted the less severe clitoridectomy-type. Heavy penalties of up to seven-year jail terms in addition to fines were imposed on midwives performing the operations. Violent disturbances accompanied the first few arrests that were made, and the British colonial government, fearing a massive nationalist revolt, eventually let the law go unendorsed. The law was ratified again in 1956, after Sudan became independent, and the punishment imposed for carrying out infibulation-type circumcision was five years imprisonment and/or a fine. However, with the introduction of the 1983 penal code, this law ceased to exist.

Whilst the current government of Sudan publicly opposes infibulation-type circumcision affirming that it is contrary to the teachings of Islam, the penal code of 1991 does not refer to FGM; as such, no law specifically outlaws the practice. Some argue, however, that FGM is covered under the codes provision on 'injury', and there have been some unconfirmed reports of arrest of practitioners.

Somalia

Prevalence rates and types of FGM carried out

The most common form of FGM practised in Somalia amongst most ethnic groups is infibulation. Clitoridectomy is practised mainly in the coastal towns of Mogadishu, Brava, Merca and Kismayu.

Virtually all Somali women are subjected to FGM, which is commonly performed on girls as young as six or seven years of age. A recent estimate by CARE International carried out in 1999 found rates of practice to be 100 per cent in one form or other.

Action on eradication

Despite the fact that the practice is so entrenched in Somali culture and custom, women began working to abolish the practice as early as 1977. The Somali Women's Democratic Organisation (SWDO), founded later that year, became the voice against FGM and was endorsed by the government. Legislation, whilst acknowledged as essential, was deemed an insufficient tool in tackling the issue. The need to gain the support of religious leaders publicly speaking out against the practice was seen as fundamental.

As one of its eradication strategies, the government supported an alternative method of circumcision – pricking the clitoris to obtain a drop of blood which, it suggested, should be carried out in hospitals to not only abolish the dangers and damage caused by traditional excisors carrying out the procedure, but also in the hope that it would replace the more dangerous infibulation. This strategy did not work as had been hoped and the practice was eventually banned in all government hospitals. A nation wide awareness-raising campaign followed, informing men and women about the health consequences of FGM, and the media was used as a tool to promote and encourage this idea of change.

In 1987, the SWDO in conjunction with the Italian Association for Woman and Development (AIDOS) launched a project to implement a campaign against infibulation. Whilst AIDOS provided technical and methodological support, SWDO was responsible for the content and direction of the campaign. Information packages were developed for dissemination to women, young people, religious leaders, and medical professionals, and by December 1987 training for trainers workshops were being run. This was followed by seminars for women, and an international conference in Mogadishu in 1989 on the theme 'Female Circumcision: Strategies to bring about change'. Firm resolutions were agreed upon with the full backing of the Somali Revolutionary Party, the ruling government of that time, which in 1988 launched a major government campaign to abolish the practice completely on health and religious grounds. The campaign maintained the operation was dangerous to women's health and contrary to the teachings of the Qur'an. At the beginning of 1991, however, this party was overthrown, leading to a major setback and an end to the positive initiatives and good work that had been achieved by the SWDO.

Recently, some international agencies have again begun anti-FGM educational campaigns, attempting to enlist women and religious leaders in the fight against the practice. Religious leaders have, in some instances, been encouraged to persuade communities that the practice is cultural and not a religious requirement. Since 1996, UNICEF in Somalia has supported a series of awareness-raising seminars attended by women's grassroots organisations, religious leaders, politicians, health professionals and other representatives of the population. In 1997, the government of Somaliland, in collaboration with UNICEF and other agencies, organised a national seminar on FGM with the aim of establishing an inter-sectoral committee at a national level and a regional task force to develop policies on eradication of the practice. UNICEF also sponsored workshops in Mogadishu, Galgaddud, Mudug and Hargeisa during 1999 and 2000. At the last workshop, participants developed a Somaliland declaration calling on the government and the people of Somaliland to abolish the practice of FGM nationally.

Current legislation on FGM

Although the former government's policy was for the complete eradication of FGM, this policy was never translated into law. There are, however, some provisions within the penal code of the former government, covering 'hurt', 'grievous hurt', and 'very grievous hurt', which might be applicable to FGM. Some regions have begun to address the issue at a local level; for example, in November 1999, the parliament of the Puntland administration unanimously approved legislation outlawing the practice.

East Africa

Kenya

Prevalence rates and types of FGM carried out

Clitoridectomy and excision-type circumcision are most commonly performed forms of circumcision, though infibulation is found in the far eastern areas bordering Somalia. A 1998 Demographic and Health Survey indicated a 38 per cent prevalence amongst Kenyan women. Though not practised amongst Kenya's two largest ethnic groups, FGM occurs at varying rates within 30 of the 40 plus ethnic groups.

Action on eradication

The Kenya National Committee on Traditional Practices (KNCTP) founded in 1990 by the United Nations Children's Fund (UNICEF) and the United Nations Development Programme (UNDP), has been working in collaboration with various other organisations including CARE/Kenya, the WHO, PATH (Programme for Appropriate Technology in Health), the International Federation of Women Lawyers (FIDA), and Maendeleo Ya Wanawake Organisation (MYWO) – which has been one of the most active groups on the issue of FGM. Since 1991, MYWO has been involved in carrying out quantitative research in four districts, and working with local communities to implement a number of strategies reflecting the findings of this research. MYWO is opposed to outlawing the practice, on the grounds that this would drive it underground. Rather, its efforts have focused on education-based approaches, i.e. informing the community on the dangers of the practice, and also developing alternative initiation rites to effect change. One such example is in the Meru district, where girls having been secluded in the traditional way, were given a week-long training on reproductive health issues, including pregnancy and HIV/AIDS prevention and information on the harmful effects of FGM. Following this, the usual community celebrations and gift-giving ceremonies followed, and the girls were given a booklet containing the communities expected code of conduct and traditions. This project – through being flexible and acknowledging community's cultural values, was welcomed by various community groups as an alternative to FGM.

Other methods of communication have included radio campaigns and the school curriculum. The Ministry of Education, which oversees the Federal Institute for Curriculum Development and Research, has made it a requirement to include educational materials discouraging harmful traditional practices, including FGM, in primary school curricula.

In March 1997, UNICEF organised a meeting to share information and co-ordinate a campaign to abolish the practice of FGM in Kenya. It was agreed that steps should be taken to outlaw the practice, whilst acknowledging that information, instruction and persuasion are the only effective tools for changing the practice.

In 1990, the Minister for Cultural and Social Services announced at an international seminar in Nairobi, that it was the government's aim to outlaw the practice. In June 1999, the Ministry of Health prepared a

National Plan of Action for the Elimination of FGM. The Director of Medical Services demanded that all government hospitals and mission hospitals cease carrying out this practice or face prosecution.

Current legislation on FGM

The prohibition of FGM is one of the measures contained in the Children's Bill passed by parliament in 2001. In August 2000, 30 people from the Tharaka district of Kenya were prosecuted by a court for secretly subjecting their daughters to FGM during the school holidays. They were each fined 2, 000 Kenyan Shillings or a prison sentence of two months in prison (Ghana Review International, 2001).

Uganda

Prevalence rates and types of FGM carried out

FGM is practised in Type I and Type II form and affects approximately 5 per cent of Ugandan females. It is found amongst the Sabiny and Pokot ethnic groups, who carry it out on girls between the ages of fourteen and sixteen.

Action on eradication

Outside efforts to bring about reform in the early 1990s, through a film portraying the mass circumcision of girls, outraged the local community because of the way the film portrayed their culture as barbaric and backward. In 1994, twice as many girls as in 1992 opted for circumcision, which is believed by many to have been a reaction to outside interference. By 1997, however, there was a radical change. The astonishing turn-around has been brought about by a UN population fund sponsored programme known as REACH (Reproductive and Community Health), whose anti-FGM efforts involved replacing FGM with alternative symbolic ritual. The main key to the success, however, lies in the collaborative partnership established between the REACH project and the traditional chiefs of the region (the Sabiny Elders association). The elders themselves undertook a methodical review of the traditional practice and, having agreed it was a destructive tradition, set about reforming it. REACH worked in close collaboration with them in helping to create an alternative ceremony by retaining the positive aspects of the occasion, such as the feasting and giving of gifts, and discarding the harmful practices. Work has also been done to improve reproductive health services and resources, and community seminars and workshops are regularly held, as are health worker training events.

Since 1996, evaluative research findings have indicated a 36 per cent decrease in the practice and, in areas where more intensive programmes have been run, the decrease has been as high as 90 per cent. The key factors in the success of this project have included strong community partnerships from the very beginning of the project, acknowledging and building on the positive cultural values, addressing FGM within a fuller reproductive health agenda, UN funding and support, and use of culturally appropriate, persuasive approaches.

Current legislation on FGM

There is currently no specific law against the practice of FGM in Uganda. In 1996, however, a court intervened to prevent the performance of the procedure on a young girl under Section 8 of the Children Statute, enacted in 1996, which makes it unlawful to subject a child to social or customary practices that are harmful to the child's health. Moves to pass a law specifically outlawing FGM are currently being considered.

United Republic of Tanzania

Prevalence rates and types of FGM carried out

According to the Demographic and Health Survey of 1996, prevalence of FGM was found to be approximately 18 per cent. Excision and infibulation are more commonly carried out, although the latter tends to be performed by Somali settlers and refugees. Incidence varies across regions and in some parts it is not carried out at all. Areas affected include Arusha, Dodoma, Mara, Kilimanjaro, Iringa, Singida, Kilosa and Mtwara. In some parts of Tanzania, 'mass circumcisions' are carried out in which thousands of girls are genitally mutilated at the same time. A 1999 report by the Tanzanian Media Women's Association estimated that 25 girls out of the 6,000 who undergo the operation every year die as a result.

Action on eradication

Campaigns against FGM in Tanzania have been complicated by lack of local and central government backing, as well as an absence of police and public support, due to a strong cultural adherence to the practice. Campaigners, when spreading information locally, have at times been subjected to attack and consequently not been able to work. As a result, they have been lobbying the government to take more effective action.

Current legislation on FGM

A law on FGM in the United Republic of Tanzania was adopted in 1998 under the Tanzanian Sexual Offences Special Provisions Act (an amendment to the penal code), specifically prohibiting FGM. The penalty for those who allow the practice to be carried out on minors in their care is imprisonment of up to fifteen years, a fine of up to 300, 000 shillings or both imprisonment and a fine. The law also provides for the payment of compensation by the perpetrator to the victim of the offence. However, in 2001, a feminist organisation Equality Now launched a protest action against the Tanzanian government on the basis that the law is not being enforced and mass circumcisions are continuing openly. Whilst some local government officials claim to have begun combating the practice, in reality, there have yet to be any prosecutions. Of the few adults who have been tried, all have been acquitted, usually because daughters have been unwilling to testify against their parents.

West Africa

Benin

Prevalence rates and types of FGM carried out
Excision-type circumcision is practised by 30 per cent of females in Benin according to a 1992 IAC survey. It is found amongst the Bariba, Peul, Boko, Baatonau, Wama, and Nago ethnic groups. Geographically, the practice is not uniformly distributed throughout the country but is more commonly carried out in the northern regions.

Action on eradication
The IAC, founded in Benin in 1982, is the leading NGO in the fight against the practice. It has conducted workshops and seminars for religious and community leaders, mayors, doctors, midwives, social workers and representatives of youth and women's organisations. A pilot project was also carried out in villages in the north of Benin by women specially trained for the project who visit and inform of the harmful health effects of the practice. The campaign has adopted a holistic approach to tackling the issue and, as such, treats the problem as a community issue involving both men and women. Medical, economic and social aspects of the practice have been the main focal points, rather than the issue of male domination, or the repression of female sexuality.

IAC also works in collaboration with the Ministry of Social Affairs and Health and the government has provided the freedom to distribute posters and informational materials in government-run clinics. The government's position on the issue of FGM is that it is committed to eliminating the practice. Whilst some government initiated activities have been channelled to rural areas through health workers informing communities about the harmful effects of the practice, it is not outlawed. Many have criticised the government, believing it has had very minimal involvement in the whole campaign against the practice.

Current legislation on FGM

There is no law explicitly criminalising the practice of FGM in Benin. The decree outlawing facial scarification from 1967 falls short of guaranteeing the integrity of the body. IAC is working to ensure that the Family Court will look at addressing this gap in the near future, and members of the National Network for the Elimination of Genital Mutilations (Reseau National de Lutte Contre les Mutilations Genitales) are working with the Ministry of Women's Affairs and Social Welfare on a proposal to outlaw the practice.

Burkina Faso

Prevalence rates and types of FGM carried out

Excision-type circumcision is practised throughout Burkina Faso, in all but a few of the 50 ethnic groups. Results from the 1999 Demographic and Health Survey (DHS) indicated that 71.6 per cent of the women have experienced FGM.

Action on eradication

Attempts to address the practice of excision have met with strong resistance from the population as a whole. The campaign against excision, launched in 1975, using radio as a means of accessing all communities, met with such hostility from communities that it was discontinued. From a survey carried out to look at attitudes towards FGM by both men and women in the community, it was agreed that any eradication campaign should focus on the medical and physical complications. Following a visit from a French human rights organisation in 1983, the late President Sankara gave a radical address to women, advising them not to rely on men to liberate them, but to have the determination to secure their own liberty. No substantive action, however, took place until May 1990, when a National Committee to Combat the Practice of Female Circumcision was created by a presidential decree. Since then the government has been engaged in an active anti-FGM campaign led by a National Committee to Fight Against the Practice of Excision (CNLPE), with Burkina Faso's First Lady as the honorary chairperson.

The National Committee operates under the administration of the Ministry for Social Action and the Family, but maintains autonomy in its activities. Its role is to oversee all work going on in the fight against FGM at a national level, and to mobilise resources, promote research, collect and publish relevant data about the practice, and monitor and evaluate activities. It has lobbied and succeeded in getting the government, not only to identify the issue as a public health priority, but also to adopt reports prepared by the Committee as official government texts, and to commit to a financial budget for its eradication.

At the core of the National Committee's work, has been the implementation of specific training sessions for each National and Provincial Committee member, and a variety of different professions, including traditional leaders, Islamic associations, churches and pastors, women's associations, health professionals, birth attendants, police, teachers, youth and press/media. Following the training, each group is asked to develop strategies to fight the practice, and this has led to a diverse range of initiatives being carried out at many different levels. Traditional leaders have organised seminars and awareness sessions at the village and family levels. Religious leaders have spoken out against the practice during services and special ceremonies. Young people have developed plays and radio campaigns aimed at spreading information about the practice to other young people. The police have established files on known excisors and, in some cases, the National Committee has provided them with training about the issue.

A 24-hour SOS telephone hotline has also been established, to inform people about the harmful effects and also to report cases of suspected or actual circumcision. In cases where the excision has not yet occurred, committee members visit the families and, if it has already occurred, the parents and excisor are served notice to report to the police. Whilst this campaign has led to some change with regards to the practice of FGM, a lack of financial support has slowed things down. In addition, some parents who are reluctant to let go of the practice have begun to have their daughters excised at birth when the operation is less likely to be noticed.

Current legislation on FGM

Since 1996, FGM has been outlawed in Burkina Faso. Under the law, excisors and accomplices continuing with the practice risk a prison sentence of six months to three years and/or a 150, 000 to 900, 000 franc fine. In cases of death following FGM, the prison sentence is five to ten years.

Since the adoption of this law, there have been 60 convictions of both excisors and accomplices, which have resulted in sentences of imprisonment or fines.

Cameroon

Prevalence rates and type of FGM carried out
According to WHO estimates, FGM reportedly affects 20 per cent of all Cameroonian women. Excision and sunna type circumcision are the types of circumcision carried out and the practice on pre-adolescent girls is found in the southwest and far north provinces.

Action on eradiacation
The National Committee of IAC actively campaigns against this practice and is supported by the government.The government has also been active against the practice through the Ministry of Women's and Social Affairs. In addition, the state-run television and newspaper have programmes and articles about this practice. A public campaign to abolish this practice within 15 to 20 years was started in March 1997.

Current legislation on FGM
There is currently no specific law on FGM in Cameroon, though women's groups and the IAC have been lobbying for legislation for a number of years.

Chad

Prevalence rates and type of FGM carried out
Excision-type circumcision is the most common form of FGM in Chad, prevalent in all parts of the country and practised by Muslims, Christians, and Animists. Infibulation is also found in the eastern part of the country in areas bordering Sudan.A 1995 United Nations report on FGM in Africa estimated that 60 per cent of the women in Chad have undergone one of these procedures.

Action on eradication
The government of Chad has enabled and supported NGOs to undertake long-term programmes to tackle the issue of FGM and has provided funding to support eradication initiatives. Whilst ASTBEF (Chadian Association for Family Wellbeing) has been the leading NGO active in combating the practice, other NGOs have organised conferences, debates and education programmes around the issue.The IAC is active in outreach programmes and the WHO has been active in mobilising the government to challenge the practice. The media has also played a major role in publicising the adversities associated with the practice and, as a result, public awareness is growing.

Current legislation on FGM

Although there is no law that specifically criminalises the practice of FGM in Chad, jurists claim that under the existing Penal Code, the practices are prosecutable as an involuntary physical assault against a minor. A new law went before Parliament in 2001, but no laws are yet in place.

The Gambia

Prevalence rates and types of FGM carried out

All four types of circumcision can be found in the Gambia, with clitoridectomy and excision-type being the most common form. Estimates of prevalence rates range from 60 to 90 per cent, and the age at which it is carried out varies from below five years to eighteen years of age.

Action on eradication

Since 1991, the Gambian NGO BAFROW (Foundation for Research on Women's Health, Production and the Environment) has been leading on the issue of FGM. Its anti-FGM programme began with a research initiative into current practices. Results of this were used to recreate a substitute ceremony 'initiation without mutilation', which was introduced to communities through outreach efforts. Political support was also sought. Results from this initiative were positive and indicated a drop in the rate of FGM in the targeted areas, as well as a rise in support from women for the abolition of the practice. A group of circumcisors trained in the new curriculum have gone on to establish their own group entitled the 'Association of Ex-circumcisors for a Better Life.' The success of this project has been attributed to the integrated collaborative approach to working with communities, as well as capacity building with partner organisations. Of primary importance, was the long-standing community trust in BAFROW, which has a long history of good community relations, having worked on various issues facing the community.

The Gambian Committee against Traditional Practices (GAMCOTRAP) is the National Committee of the IAC, which has taken on the lead role of informing the public about the harmful effects of traditional practices including FGM. Various strategies have been used at the grassroots level, and training workshops and programmes have been used to provide information on the harmful effects of the practice to women, community leaders, youth and children. Lectures are held around the country to reach a wider audience. As a result, the once taboo subject is now openly discussed. A symposium for religious leaders and medical personnel on FGM as a form of violence was also organised by GAMCOTRAP, resulting in the Banjul Declaration of July 22, 1998, which condemned the continuation of the practice, declaring it as having neither Islamic nor Christian origins, nor any other justification.

Current legislation on FGM
There is no specific law in the Gambia that outlaws this practice.

Ghana

Prevalence rates and types of FGM carried out
According to estimates by the Gender Studies and Human Rights Documentation Centre, the prevalence rate of FGM in Ghana in 1998 was 15 per cent. The predominant form of circumcision practised is excision-type, though clitoridectomy is also carried out in some regions. Geographically, FGM is more commonly found in the upper east regions, but is also found elsewhere. Both Muslims and Christians carry it out in a number of ethnic groups including Kussasi, Frafra, Kassena, Nankanne, Bassauri, Moshie, Manprusie, Kantansi, Walas, Sissala, Grunshie, Dargati and Lobi.

Action on eradication
The government of Ghana has spoken out against the practice at all levels, and this has created an environment supportive of the efforts of NGOs. The most successful of the programmes to date have been the collaborative efforts of the Ghana Association for Women's Welfare (GAWW) and the Muslim Family and Counselling Services (MFGMS). GAWW, founded in 1984, is a charter member of the IAC. Both have been successful and have received invitations to speak in communities about the practice and work with local leaders (community, ethnic and political) to organise and conduct workshops on the issue. They have worked with the leaders ensuring that their role and support is prominent in the process. This groundwork has made the entire community receptive and has assured a positive attendance at GAWW/MFGMS workshops held throughout the country. Participants of the workshop are given information on the harmful effects of the practice, the laws prohibiting it, and the absence of Qur'anic imperatives for it. All topics are addressed in an open forum where questions and comments are encouraged. Workshops for former excisors have also been held to help them find other work.

Current legislation on FGM

In 1989, the head of the government of Ghana, President Rawlings, issued a formal declaration against FGM and other harmful traditional practices. In 1994, parliament amended the criminal code of 1960 to include FGM as a specific offence.

There have been seven arrests under the Act since 1994 and at least two practitioners have been prosecuted and convicted. For example, in March 1995, police arrested and charged the practitioner and parents of an eight-year-old girl who had been circumcised, and in June 1998, a practitioner was sentenced to three years in prison for having performed this procedure on three girls. Some are of the opinion, however, that the law has driven the practice underground and that education at the grassroots is crucial to changing superstitions, attitudes and beliefs.

Guinea

Prevalence rates and types of FGM carried out

The 1999 Demographic Health Survey outlined an FGM prevalence rate of 98.6 per cent. Type I, II and III are all practised, and found in particular amongst the Peul, Malinke, Coussou, Guerza, Toma and Nalou ethnic groups.

Action on eradication

Established in 1988, the NGO La Cellule de Co-ordination sur les Pratiques Traditionelles Affectan la sante des Femmes et des Enfants (CPTAFE) has rolled out a national eradication programme against FGM. This work is mainly based on voluntary efforts by key community leaders including religious leaders, teachers, journalists, and health workers. Each region devises its own local response under the supervision and co-ordination of the national office, which ensures that there is some degree of consistency and sharing of good practice across all regions. An important factor, which drives all local initiatives, is the local research carried out to establish cultural norms, local beliefs, and customs of each area so as to tailor programmes accordingly. Effective education and outreach work is deemed an essential component in the journey towards eradication, which cannot be achieved solely through legal measures. It is recognised that media coverage sensationalises the practice and can also be damaging, and efforts, therefore, are made to engage the media in a meaningful way to enhance the work being done.

In 1999, opponents of FGM in Guinea welcomed the decision by hundreds of circumcisors to hand in their special ceremonial knives.

The handing-in ceremony took place in Korosa, and was regarded as a significant breakthrough after fourteen years of campaigning.

Current legislation on FGM

FGM is illegal in Guinea under Article 265 of the Penal Code. The punishment is hard labour for life and, if death results within 40 days after the crime, the perpetrator will be sentenced to death. However, no cases regarding the practice under the law have ever been brought to trial. A member of the Guinean Supreme Court is working with a local NGO on inserting a clause into the Guinean Constitution specifically prohibiting these practices.

Guinea Bissau

Prevalence rates and types of FGM carried out

Although widespread in Guinea-Bissau, prevalence of Type I and Type II FGM varies from area to area and amongst ethnic groups. It is commonly practised in one or other form amongst the Mandinkas and Peul groups. Estimates of overall prevalence have noted considerable variation in incidence between urban (70-80 per cent prevalence) and rural (20-30 per cent prevalence) areas.

Action on eradication

The debate on FGM started in the early 1980s in Guinea-Bissau. Action started with the establishment of the National Committee for the Elimination of Harmful Practices against Women and Children, set up by the government in the early 1990s. Against a background of slow progress, Sinim Mira Nassigue – an NGO, was established by a group of Guinean women and men committed to the cause. Despite limits in funding, it established support centres in a number of regions and members go from house to house to sensitise the communities about the harmful consequences of FGM. The organisation emphasises the importance of including the 'fanatecas' (the circumcisors) in the process since they have strong commercial interests in maintaining the practice, whilst also having high social status. Sinim Mira Nassigue recently supervised a 'fanado modelo', an alternative initiation rite for 35 young girls, during which all the traditional parts of the ceremony were followed but without the girls being circumcised.

The Guinean government gives some support to groups conducting educational seminars on FGM. Sinim Mira Nassigue, however, has developed as a main driving force in this fight.

Current legislation on FGM

In 1995, a government proposal to outlaw FGM was defeated in parliament, although it was upheld that circumcisors would be held criminally responsible should FGM lead to any cases of death.

The Ivory Coast

Prevalence rates and types of FGM carried out

According to UNICEF, some four million women have undergone a form of FGM in the Ivory Coast, and the practice is found particularly amongst the rural populations in the northern, central and western parts of the country. Results of a 1999 Demographic and Health Survey, which included 3,040 women nationally, indicated 45 per cent of women to have been excised.

Action on eradication

The Association for International Development in Africa (AIDF) has worked extensively with local women's committees, religious leaders and the government to raise awareness of the health issues related to the practice. Seminars have been held for circumcisors, national and local political and administrative authorities, traditional chiefs and police officers and gendarmes on the negative consequences of this practice. At a June 1996 AIDF seminar, the practice was exposed as a moneymaking activity for village excisors. The seminar led to the establishment of a National Committee to fight the practice, chaired by the Ministry of Women's Affairs and Family, and run by a former excisor who abandoned the practice after having performed operations for 40 years.

The government and various national and international organisations such as AIDF, UNICEF, Amnesty International, and the Federation of the Red Cross have also held several seminars between 1996 and 1998 for communities as well as doctors, lawyers, and religious leaders. With an outcry against the unsanitary conditions associated with FGM, attempts have been made to have the procedure carried out in hospitals and dispensaries, although AIDF has continued to fight against medicalising the practice, believing that this sends out the wrong message.

A number of professional bodies including the Gynaecological and Obstetrical Society, the National Federation of Midwives and the Association for the Wellbeing of the Family have campaigned against the practice using radio and the press. In 1998, in response to the collective campaign and pressures, AIDF together with various other

NGOs and traditional and religious authorities that have generally upheld the practice, began to take part in public demonstrations against it. Although the process of change is slow, as women and girls become more aware of the harmful health effects through the numerous campaigns of information and education, things may change.

Current legislation on FGM
In December 1998, genital excision became a punishable offence in the Ivory Coast, for which a jail term of five years could be imposed, as well as fines of between 360, 000 – 2 million francs. In cases where excision leads to death, jail sentences are increased to twenty years.

Liberia

Prevalence rates and types of FGM carried out
Type II and, to a lesser degree, Type I FGM are reportedly practised in most parts of Liberia by three groups and, according to the Inter Parliamentary Union (IPU), estimates in 1984, indicate prevalence rates to be between 50 and 70 per cent. Type II tends to be practised by the Gola and Kisil ethnic groups.

Action on eradication
In 1985 the Liberian National Committee, in affiliation with the IAC on Traditional Practices Affecting the Health of Women and Children, was set up to conduct research into the prevention of FGM and attitudes towards the custom. In collaboration with the Ministry of Health and Social Affairs, efforts were made to integrate awareness of the consequences of the practice into programmes for mothers on childcare, and primary health care. During the civil crisis, the IAC National Committee continued its awareness-raising programmes with rural women, students in secondary schools, religious leaders, women's groups and youth groups, providing training about the harmful effects of this practice. Extensive media campaigns were also carried out. Income generating training was provided for a number of excisors with the aim of diverting them to other sources of income generation.

Since 1994, the Committee has tried to incorporate biblical teachings into its campaigns, with the aim of getting more support from elders and chiefs within the community. Little is believed to have changed and support from government officials is still felt to be lacking.

Current legislation on FGM
There is no specific law in Liberia that makes the practice of FGM illegal. Under Section 242 of the Penal Code, however, a person can be

found guilty and imprisoned for up to five years if he or she:

> *maliciously and unlawfully injures another by cutting off or otherwise depriving him of any of the members of his body*

No cases, however, have yet been reported under this provision.

Mali

Prevalence rates and types of FGM carried out

Clitoridectomy, excision, and infibulation-type circumcision are found in Mali, though the former two are the most common. A 1999 Demographic Health Survey reported 93 per cent of women to have undergone the practice. Whilst in the past this practice was part of the marriage ceremony and was performed on girls aged fourteen and fifteen, more recently the custom has changed and it tends to be carried out much earlier.

Action on eradication

Outreach activities concerning this practice have been carried out for many years. 1984 saw the establishment of the Comite Malien de Lutte Contres Les Pratiques Traditionnelles Nefastes (COMAPRAT) which has provided programmes on the health effects of the practice for midwives and religious leaders. Following a change of government in 1990, this organisation was dissolved and replaced by the IAC organisation, Association Malienne pour le Suivi et l'Orientation des Pratiques Traditionnelles (AMSOPT). This has carried out projects on the harmful effects of the practice with youth, religious leaders and excisors throughout Mali. Since 1991, a number of NGOs have been active in their efforts to inform people about the practice. In addition, a number of local women have set up organisations to address the issue by raising awareness amongst women, and running eradication campaigns through a number of methods. Theatre has been found to be a popular and effective vehicle for getting messages across and changing attitudes. A travelling troupe of dancers and actors have put on performances about serious development and health issues in villages, using humour and music in a way that have never been seen before in theatre; the issue of FGM has been tackled head on, illustrating the medical dangers and social taboos. Following a performance in a village called Mana, the chief of the village emulated his theatrical counterpart in the performance by announcing that now that they understood the dangers of circumcision the village would put a stop to the practice. The following morning, sitting in his compound surrounded by village elders, the chief repeated this pledge but also quoted a Bambara proverb realising that things would not change overnight.

In 1996, the government formed a National Action Committee to promote the eradication of harmful health practices against women and children through the development of coherent strategies leading to concrete action. This committee, comprised of government representatives from each Ministry, as well as representatives from NGOs, national health and science research institutions and the religious community, engage in activities to share information and raise public awareness, through production of audio-visual materials, training, promotion of research, legislation reform, and support of NGOs set up to combat these harmful practices.

Following a national seminar on strategies to abolish FGM in June 1997, a plan of action for the eradication of FGM by 2007 was outlined. The first phase of the plan was to establish a database on the practice, develop and implement eradication programmes, and establish better co-ordination between national and international organisations.

Current legislation on FGM

To date, the government response has been to support campaigns against the practice but not to outlaw it. Provisions in the code outlawing assault and grievous bodily harm arguably cover this practice, and the government has also stated that the practice is prohibited under Articles 166 and 171 of the Penal Code covering voluntary strikes or wounds and harmful experimental treatments, respectively. However, following the recommendations made at the national seminar in 1997, the government did charge the National Action Committee to submit draft legislation to the National Assembly to specifically outlaw the practice. So far, however, no specific law has been passed, and local resistance to eliminating the practice is thought to be one of the reasons why the legislation has not got through.

Mauritania

Prevalence rates and types of FGM carried out

The Mauritanian Ministry of Health has estimated the prevalence of FGM at between 20 and 25 per cent. Types of FGM practised include Type I, II and also Type IV. Ethnic groups practising FGM include the Pulaar, Soninke, Toucouleurs, Moors, and Wolof, and incidence within these ethnic groups is varied.

Action on eradication

It was not until the 1970s that FGM was spoken against and brought onto the mainstream agenda in Mauritania for the first time. NGOs and public health workers have provided education and information to women about the harmful effects, as well as pointing out that it is not a religious requirement. In1997 the Secretary of State for Women's Affairs formed a committee to co-ordinate activities against the practice. UNICEF and UNFPA are also working on a number of projects. An eminent Imam who is a member of the higher Islamic Council of Mauritania, has also been a prominent figure in the campaign, advocating that that the practice is not a religious requirement in Islam.

Current legislation on FGM

Whilst the practice is not outlawed, it is banned in hospitals.

Niger

Prevalence rates and types of FGM carried out

According to 1998 Demographic and Health Survey figures, the prevalence rate of FGM in Niger was 5 per cent. Type I and II are the most commonly practised forms of circumcision, and Type III is rare. FGM is generally carried out amongst the Shouna, Kanuris, Zarma-Sonrhais, Peul, Songhai, Kourtey and Wago ethnic groups.

Action on eradication

A government decree in 1990 established the Committee against Harmful Traditional Practices (Lutte Contra les Practices Traditionnelles Nefastes or CONIPRAT) to campaign against the practice by carrying out publicity campaigns to raise awareness, by disseminating information on the practice in local languages, and by participating in research. This has become the leading NGO in the fight against FGM. The government is engaged firmly in an effort to eliminate the practice and in March 1997 the Minister of Health announced that the government would do whatever it could to halt the practice of FGM. The government works closely with other local NGOs, the United Nations Children's Fund, and others to develop and distribute educational materials at clinics and health centres. Several seminars have also been organised with the aim of raising awareness at regional and local levels. In one rural area, excisors turned in their knives and pledged to discontinue the practice of FGM, a motion that received prominent coverage in the media.

Current legislation on FGM

FGM is not outlawed in its own right under the Penal Code although jurists unanimously equate it with the intentional assault described in and punishable by Article 222 of the code, whereby offenders are subject to a minimum of three months to two years imprisonment and/or a 100,000 francs fine. In 1999, the Ministry of Social Development, Population, Advancement of Women and Protection of Children prepared a bill outlawing FGM and providing a heavier prison term of three to twenty years. It has not yet been debated and adopted by parliament.

Nigeria

Prevalence rates and types of FGM carried out

A national survey into the practice of FGM in Nigeria by the National Association of Nigerian Nurses and Midwives (NANNM) in 1985 and 1986 revealed that all 4 types are found there, and carried out in one form or other by all religious groups, and the majority of ethnic groups, in thirteen of the twenty-one states. The Yoruba, Ibo, Ijaw, Hausa, and Kanuri make up some of the larger ethnic groups that practise it.

Action on eradication

Efforts to carry out anti-FGM work in Nigeria have existed since the late 1970s, when a Nigerian journalist undertook a comprehensive campaign to tackle the issue from a medical and health point of view as opposed to one demanding individuals to question their longstanding cultural or religious beliefs. She outlined the importance of data collection to establish incidence of the practice and the methods used to carry out the operations, and she concluded that eradication programmes needed to target individuals at maternity clinics, women's societies, schools and colleges, hospitals, nursing and medical schools. She also felt that legislation was not an effective tool in eradication, and rather served to push the practice more underground.

The National Association of Nigerian Nurses and Midwives (NANNM) received funding in the early 1990s to run an eradication programme in eleven states. The aims of the project were to train health workers to identify the different types of FGM, and to empower them to teach other professionals, as well as the community, about the harmful effects. A number of methods were used to achieve these aims, including educational campaigns in markets, televised dramas, visits to community and social groups, meetings with traditional and religious leaders, and working with community members to develop educational materials. In 1995, the project was evaluated through reviews of documents developed through the project, and a series of interviews with key people including circumcisors. Although no comparative data was collected, results from the evaluation suggested that the project had had some impact on raising awareness of the harmful effects amongst health workers and the general public, and reducing, to some degree, the incidence of FGM. The main determining factors essential to the project, were working in collaboration with local community leaders and involving communities in the design, implementation, and monitoring of the initiatives. Lack of government involvement and short life projects were felt to have been barriers to progress.

Current legislation on FGM

Currently, there is no specific law banning the practice of FGM in Nigeria. Opponents of these practices rely on Section 34(1)(a) of the 1999 Constitution of the Federal Republic of Nigeria as the basis for banning the practice. This states that:

> *no person shall be subjected to torture or inhuman or degrading treatment*

Since 1999, however, six of the 36 States, including Edo State (where a conviction was recently made resulting in a 1,000 Naira fine and six months' imprisonment), have illegalised the practice. The IAC in Nigeria is pursuing a state-by-state strategy to criminalise the practice in all 36 states. The campaign is expected to take at least five years to reach all 36 states. Nigeria is, however, looking to pass a federal law on violence against women, which will cover FGM and will protect all females in Nigeria.

Senegal

Prevalence rates and types of FGM carried out

Type II and III FGM affects about one-fifth of females in this West African country, according to a 1988 study by the Environmental Development Action in the Third World (ENDA). Ethnic groups that practise a form of FGM include Toucouleur, Sarakole, Peul, Bambara, Halpular, Mande, Diolas, Mandingos, and the Tenda.

Action on eradication

The Commission Internationals pour l'Abolition des Mutilation Sexuelle (CAMS) has been working in Senegal since 1982 to help abolish the practice and set up a gender research unit on women at the University of Dakar.

In 1991, the NGO Tostan, with the financial backing of the UN Children's Fund, began a non-formal education programme for women in more than 450 villages. One of its main aims was to encourage the empowerment of women. Methods used included games, small group discussions, theatre, songs, dance, story telling and flip charts. The modules covered included literacy skills, problem solving, women's health and hygiene, management skills, leadership skills, negotiating skills and human rights. From the outset, Tostan did not dwell on the issue of FGM or state whether it was a good or bad practice. In a number of cases, the women themselves, after taking the programme, decided that they no longer wanted their daughters to be subjected to this practice and used the skills learned in the programme to approach their husbands and village leaders to ask for the practice to stop. For example, in 1997, the village of Malicounda Bambara (which has a population of 3,000) decided to abandon the practice as a result of the efforts of a number of women who, with the support of local Imams, took the initiative to inform other women, men and children in the village and in neighbouring villages about the harmful health effects.

In February 1998, former President Diouf appealed for an end to this practice and called for legislation to outlaw it. He supported the initiative by a group of women from a small village east of Dakar who launched a campaign backed by religious leaders to wipe out the practice. For him, this was an example that could be followed by the rest of the country.

Following the accession to power of President Abdoulaye Wade in March 2000, a new study was proposed to review the current extent of the practice, to assess the impact of Senegal's 1999 law, and to develop an integrated governmental approach in conjunction with all groups working against the practice.

Current legislation on FGM

The law passed in 1999, illegalising FGM, modifies the Penal Code to make this practice a criminal act, punishable by a sentence of one to five years in prison. Since the law was passed, there has been at least one case which led to the arrest of eight women and five elderly men who were sentenced to three years' imprisonment for permitting or assisting with the circumcision of eighteen young girls in the Kolda district of Senegal. The arrest, however, sparked off outrage and threats of violence by other village elders from the region, and many feel that legislation will drive the practice further underground.

Sierra Leone

Prevalence rates and types of FGM carried out

Excision-type circumcision is the form widely practised on women and girls in Sierra Leone, occurs amongst all ethnic and religious groups with the exception of the Krios. Various estimates suggest an 80 to 90 per cent prevalence rate.

Action on eradication

In Sierra Leone, the IAC's Association on Women's Welfare (SLAWW), was set up in 1984 to raise awareness amongst the public about the dangers of FGM, advocating for legislation to abolish the practice. Their approach has been sensitive and cautious because of the levels of local feeling against groups opposing the practice. Discussion of the practice and its problems was first initiated amongst doctors, midwives, nurses, teachers, students and journalists. Progress was made to establish alternative employment opportunities for excisors. The activities of SLAWW, however, were interrupted in May 1997 due to the political crisis during which most of its members had to flee the country, although advocacy work continued with members of other NGOs such as Marie Stopes, the YWCA, the Methodist Ministers Wives' Association, the Council of Churches of Sierra Leone and the Young Muslim Brotherhood. Other private grassroots organisations have arranged various initiatives such as teaching for community groups and primary and secondary school teachers about the dangers of FGM and ways to abolish it. A National Drama Group in late 2000 also performed a play discouraging FGM, which was attended by the President and other senior ministers.

Current legislation on FGM

Currently, there is no specific law prohibiting FGM in Sierra Leone.

Togo

Prevalence rates and types of FGM carried out

Excision-type circumcision occurs in four of Togo's five predominant regions. In a study carried out in 1996 by the Demographic Research Unit, prevalence was found to be approximately 12 per cent, with considerable variation across regions. The practice of FGM crosses all religious and most ethnic groups including Cotocoli, Tchamba, Peul, Mossi, Yanga, Moba, Gourma and Ana-Ife.

Action on eradication

IAC Togo, formed in 1984 with the support of the Ministry of Social Affairs, has carried out work with communities, excisors, health workers, and policy-makers through seminars and workshops.

In 1997, a major campaign was started in the central region, an area of high incidence. The aim was to inform various professional groups, including political and administrative groups, traditional and religious authorities, and students about the harmful effects. In a campaign carried out by the German Volunteer Service (DED), twenty-five excisors were encouraged to go through an awareness-raising programme and subsequently pledged to stop their practice. A project to look at alternative income producing activities was also run.

Various human rights and women's rights groups in Togo also have outreach programmes targeting rural populations, educating them about the health dangers of this practice. According to a senior Togolese human rights activist, such programmes are having limited immediate success and it will take a long time before a reduction in the practice is seen.

Current legislation on FGM

On 30 October 1998, the National Assembly in Togo unanimously voted to outlaw the practice of FGM, after the parliamentary human rights commission said the practice attacked women's physical integrity and was not justified on religious or cultural grounds. Penalties under the law can include a prison term from two months to ten years and a fine of between 100,000 to 1,000,000 francs. A person who knows that the procedure is going to take place and fails to inform public authorities can also be punished with anything between a month to a year's imprisonment, or a fine of 20,000 to 500,000 francs.

At least one excisor has been arrested under the law, although the outcome of this case is not yet known.

Central Africa

Central African Republic

Prevalence rates and types of FGM carried out

Excision and clitoridectomy are reportedly practised in the Central African Republic. The prevalence rate was found to be 43 per cent in the 1994 Demographic Health Survey, with eight of the ten ethnic groups following the practice. Whilst the majority of girls undergo the practice between the ages of seven and fifteen, in about 10 per cent of cases, the operation is carried out after the age of fifteen.

Action on eradication

A number of awareness-raising programmes have been organised by the Ministry of Social Welfare and NGOs including 'Women, Nutrition and Development' in 1989, which focused awareness-building campaigns on the harmful effects of excision. Little information is available on further work that has been carried out.

Current legislation on FGM

FGM has been illegal since 1966, though no cases of arrests have been reported. Legislation is thought to have had little effect, particularly in the rural areas.

Arabian Peninsula

Yemen

Prevalence rates and types of FGM carried out

The most common form of FGM practised in Yemen is excision, although infibulation is found amongst a small group of East African immigrants. According to the 1997 Yemen Demographic Mother and Child Health Survey, 23 per cent of all married Yemeni women have undergone the procedure, which occurs throughout the country at varying rates. It tends to be carried out in the home during the first month of life.

Action on eradication

FGM was publicly discussed in Yemen at the National Women's Committee (NWC) conference in July 2000. At this event, health officials including the Minister of Public Health decreed the practice should cease and established a plan of action to reduce the incidence. Religious leaders were also tasked to provide an opinion on the practice in consultation with doctors, whilst government ministers were asked to develop a public awareness campaign in areas most affected by the practice. The Minister of Public Health was asked to conduct a nation wide study to determine the extent of this problem. It was also recommended that FGM be included in the curricula at medical schools, health institutes and literacy centres.

In 2001, the Ministry of Public Health sponsored a two-day seminar entitled 'Female Health', attended by approximately 150 academics, health professionals, government officials, donors and clerics. In his opening remarks, the Minister described this practice as a form of violence against women and a violation of their human rights.

Current legislation on FGM

There is no specific law against FGM in Yemen, though a ministerial decree in January 2001 prohibited the practice in both government and private health facilities.

CHAPTER SIX

FEMALE CIRCUMCISION
IN THE UK

Introduction

This chapter looks at female circumcision in the UK. It illustrates how the practice originated, receiving wide acceptance and endorsement by the church, and then disappeared only to resurface in the 1980s following the arrival of immigrants, asylum seekers, and refugees from FGM-practising countries (such as Somalia, Sudan, Djibouti, Eritrea, Ethiopia, Sierra Leone, and Nigeria). The chapter looks at their settlements and demographic patterns in the UK, the extent of the problem, legislative developments, initiatives by non-governmental organisations (NGOs), local responses, and the work of professional bodies in tackling the issue.

The historical context

As mentioned earlier, FGM is not a non-western phenomenon, but has been practised in many civilisations and in every continent over the years. At about the same time that European travellers were learning about its existence amongst certain groups in Africa, accounts of the procedure being carried out in the West appeared in English and continental journals. As is often the case with obsolete and disreputable practices, there is little reference to FGM as a 'western practice' in western anthropological literature. There is, however, plenty of material that portrays it as a 'tribal' ritual, associated with so-called 'uncivilised', 'primitive' and 'ignorant' non-western societies.

In reality, clitoridectomy was performed on women in England up until the last century. Medical practitioners during the nineteenth century saw it as their task to promote the health and prosperity of the nation, and books and pamphlets warning against the consequences of sexual excess appeared from the 1830s onwards. In particular, growing concern mounted about masturbation, and perpetrators of this practice were perceived by some religious quarters as sexually deviant. Concern grew to such a level that by the mid 1800s, clitoridectomy and even the more severe infibulation-type form of circumcision, became widely advocated as acceptable curative techniques by medical practitioners and religious groups. Others, such as Bennett, an English gynaecologist, advocated the use of leeches in the treatment of women's hysteria, by placing them on the vulva or uterus (Feibelman, 1997). He also recommended managing the illness with cauterisation procedures e.g. by administering nitrate of silver or hydrate potassium to the inside of the uterus with a hot iron instrument.

In the first six decades of the nineteenth century, numerous accounts of de-clitorisation appeared in the Lancet. The origins of nymphomania, thought by some to be linked to the cerebellum and by others to the ovaries or uterus, also became linked to the clitoris by English obstetricians such as Samuel Ashwall who recommended excision when an enlarged clitoris gave rise to sexual passion. Such beliefs led to a wave of excision-type operations in Germany, France and England. One of the earliest accounts is that cited by Tanner (1866), who gives a detailed surgical account and an outline of behavioural assumptions prevalent in Paris from as early as 1812. He writes that:

> *A young woman was so addicted to masturbation that she became reduced to the last stage of marasmus. Sensible of the danger of her situation, yet not possessed of sufficient fortitude, or else irresistibly impelled by the pleasurable sensations which resulted, she could not command herself. If her hands were tied, she resorted to friction against the edge of the bed. If her legs were fastened, she managed by moving her thighs, to provoke abundant pollutions. Her parents took her to Professor Dubois. Following the example of Levret, he proposed amputation of the clitoris, which the patient and her parents agreed to. The organ was removed with one stroke of a bistoury, and the bleeding was prevented by an application of the actual cautery. The operation quickly succeeded, and the patient was cured of her fatal habit. She quickly recovered her health and strength.*

The practice of clitoridectomy reached its highest incidence in England in the 1860s, and became widely advocated by the highly regarded and talented surgeon Isaac Baker Brown, who advocated it for almost every kind of female pathology. *The Church Times* (a religious publication), condoned the practice describing Baker-Brown as an eminent surgeon who has published:

a little volume of cases which prove incontestably the success for
the treatment... which will enable them (the Church) to suggest a
remedy for some of the most distressing illnesses which they
frequently discover amongst their parishioners... and within the
clergy will be doing a service, especially to their poorer
parishioners, by bringing under the notice of medical men, any of
whom can, if possessed by ordinary surgical skills, perform the
operation with but a slight assistance.

Barker-Benfield, 1976

This led to one of the UK's most heated medical controversies of the nineteenth century, culminating in the eventual downfall and end of Baker-Brown's career. The practice died out in England by the end of the nineteenth century.

In the USA, both clitoridectomy and oophorectomy (removal of the ovaries) were carried out to combat masturbation and other common illnesses (Feibelman, 1997). The Reverend John Todd, a well-known writer from Massachusetts, became renowned for his outspokenness on the issue of masturbation. He recorded his views in *The Student's Manual* first published in 1835, and relaunched in 1854 for its 24th edition. Warnings against masturbation were issued in newspapers and posters following the assertion in 1848 by the superintendent of the lunatic asylum in Worcester, Massachusetts, that female masturbation was a sign of insanity and male masturbation a sign of being 'lost'. Females were more harshly condemned and were perceived as being a threat to all men (Feibelman, 1997). Such behavioural traits did not sit well with the ideal image of women at that time, as feeble, weak and dainty. In some upper-class families, these qualities were induced in wives and daughters by feeding them drops of arsenic, nitrate, or silver in order to increase their ashen, delicate pallor. Female circumcision continued to be practised in some parts of America until as late as 1937. Asefa (1994) claims that FGM, as a cure for masturbation, was practised in various western nations including Canada, England and the United States, until as recently as the 1940s to treat masturbation as well as other female 'deviances'. The findings of Ehrenreich and English (1973), also support this view:

> *the last clitoridectomy we know of in the United States was*
> *performed twenty-five years ago on a child of five, as a cure for*
> *masturbation.*

The current situation in the UK

The migration to the UK of people from FGM-practising countries (such as Somalia, Sudan, Djibouti, Eritrea, Ethiopia, Sierra Leone, and Nigeria), either as economic migrants, asylum seekers, refugees or students, has reintroduced the practice of FGM. Various professionals nationwide no doubt, are likely to encounter girls and women who have either been circumcised or are 'at risk' of being circumcised.

It is very difficult to give exact figures of circumcised females or those 'at risk' of circumcision in the UK. It is also very difficult to estimate, as the census data fails to differentiate specifically between ethnic groups, applying the categories 'black African/ black British-African' in England and Wales, and 'African' or 'black Scottish / other black' in Scotland. These general ethnic categories provide for the collective classification of nationals from fifty-three potential countries each made up of varying cultural groups, not all of which are FGM-practising. Similarly, one cannot assume that those females in the category of 'black British' or 'Scottish black' are all non-circumcised, since there is anecdotal evidence to suggest that some girls born and brought up here in the UK continue to be circumcised. The UK's African population is also a relatively under-studied social group in British race relations particularly because there has been a tendency to homogenise them under the category 'African-Caribbean' or 'black'. Furthermore, since there is no mandatory requirement or a standardised system or database to monitor or record cases of FGM, when they come to the attention of hospitals or other professionals, providing figures on the numbers of women and girls that are affected becomes very difficult.

With all the difficulties, however, a glimpse has been provided by the Foundation for Women's Health Research and Development (FORWARD), the UK's leading body working on FGM. Using census data figures as well as Home Office statistics on the numbers of immigrants, refugees, and asylum applications from countries where FGM is endemic, it has estimated that 74,000 first-generation African immigrant women in the UK have undergone FGM, and up to 20,000 women and girls are 'at risk' of circumcision (FORWARD, 1996).

FORWARD's report *Out of Sight, Out of Mind* (Read, 1998) surveyed social services departments (SSDs) and local education authorities (LEAs) reporting communities who traditionally practise FGM living within their area (see Table 1). Although not all SSDs and LEAs responded, the survey did give some indication of the number of SSDs and LEAs who may well encounter conditions in women that result from female circumcision.

Country of Origin	SSDs	LEA
Somalia	18	11
Djibouti	0	1
Ethiopia	8	7
Mali	1	0
Sudan	7	5
Sierra Leone	12	6
Burkina Faso	0	1
The Gambia	4	5
Ivory Coast	0	1
Kenya	10	7
Senegal	0	1
Egypt	7	8
Guinea	0	1
Conakry	0	0
Guinea Bissau	0	1
Nigeria	15	12
Mauritania	0	2
Central Africa	2	2
Niger	0	0
Chad	0	0
Benin	0	2
Togo	0	1
Ghana	10	8
Tanzania	6	6
Uganda	7	9
Zaire	6	7
Yemen	6	4
India	1	2
Malaysia	2	5

(Read, D., 1998)

Table 1: Number of SSDs and LEAs reporting communities who traditionally practise FC living within their LA area

Settlement and demographic composition

Africans have resided in Great Britain since antiquity. The desire to explore the source of colonisers' powers and better their employment prospects led many from West Africa – particularly from Sierra Leone, Nigeria, and the Gold Coast, and East Africans from British Somaliland to settle in the docklands of Cardiff, Liverpool, London, and other ports (Banton, 1955; Killingray, 1994). Most of them were reputed to be particularly independent and, according to Little (1948), this was probably a reflection of their nomadic clan-based socialisation. Nevertheless, before the 1950s the African population of Britain was less than 10,000 (Daley, 1996). It was not until the 1950s and 60s that further migration occurred. The post-World War Two economic climate had created labour shortages that made the British government encourage migrants from the Commonwealth to Britain. This was because under the Commonwealth rules, Commonwealth citizens had free entry into Britain. Over this period, therefore, Britain received a large number of immigrants from Asia, Africa and the Caribbean. However, the devastation of civil war and famine during the 1980s in certain parts of Africa brought further numbers of refugees, asylum seekers and economic migrants to the UK. The 2001 Census showed the black-African population at 0.8 per cent or 485,233 of the total UK population (see Table 2). The majority are concentrated in the southeast, particularly London, which has a black African population of 378,933 or 5.3 per cent of the total London population.

Country/Region	Total Population	Black African Population	% of Black Africans
United Kingdom	58,789,194	485,233	0.8
England	49,138,831	475,938	1.0
Northern Ireland	1,685,267	506	0.0
Scotland	5,062,011	5062	0.1
Wales	2,903,085	3,727	0.1
North East	2,515,442	2,597	0.1
North West	6,729,764	15,912	0.2
Yorkshire & The Humber	4,964,833	9,625	0.2
East Midlands	4,172,174	9,165	0.2
West Midlands	5,267,308	11,985	0.2
East	5,388,140	16,968	0.3
London	7,172,091	378,933	5.3
South East	8,000,645	24,582	0.3
South West	4,928,434	6,171	0.1

(ONS, 2003)

Table 2: black-African population by country and region, 2001

The majority of black-Africans live in England and make up 475,938, or 1 per cent, of the total population. In both Scotland and Wales, black-Africans make up 0.1 per cent of the total population, with 5,062 individuals in Scotland, and 3,727 in Wales. Northern Ireland has just 506 black-Africans. The gender divide is not significant, with males totalling 229,103 and females slightly higher at 246,835 (see Table 3). What is significant, however, is that 136,170 (28.6 per cent) of the total African population is aged 14 or below. Out of these, 67568 (49.5 per cent) are girls. Whilst one must be cautious in assuming that this population group is at risk of circumcision, it would also be naïve to assume that all are free from risk.

Age range	ENGLAND Total Persons	Male	Female	WALES Total Persons	Male	Female
ALL PEOPLE	475938	229103	246835	3727	1949	1778
0 to 4	50484	25745	24739	331	150	181
5 to 7	28443	14371	14072	211	119	92
8 to 10	17638	8730	8908	110	69	41
11 to 14	39605	19756	19849	293	169	124
15	7564	3774	3790	61	29	32
16 to 17	16181	7963	8218	117	52	65
18 to 19	14877	7133	7744	164	84	80
20 to 24	38218	17986	20232	375	192	183
25 to 29	46879	21169	25710	322	145	177
30 to 34	60472	27446	33026	316	170	146
35 to 39	53008	24676	28332	319	189	130
40 to 44	37689	18557	19132	242	133	109
45 to 49	21927	10773	11154	178	101	77
50 to 54	14417	6998	7419	136	68	68
55 to 59	9531	4176	5355	106	48	58
60 to 64	8204	4229	3975	115	57	58
65 to 69	4846	2712	2134	90	53	37
70 to 74	2834	1455	1379	95	45	50
75 to 79	1582	820	762	66	37	29
80 to 84	971	443	528	50	26	24
85 to 89	342	122	220	18	7	11
90 and over	226	69	157	12	6	6

(ONS, 2003)

Table 3: black-African people by age and gender in England and Wales, 2001

Legislative developments in the UK

FGM came to be noticed in the UK in the 1980s, not because of its historical presence or the migration of certain African ethnic groups, but when it became known that some private clinics in London were performing circumcision on girls and women from overseas who were requesting it. The clientele were mostly the African elite, whose custom led to huge profits for these clinics, until the media exposed them creating a public outcry. A heated debate followed in which some argued that these clinics were right to allow the procedure to be carried out under anaesthetic, in sterile conditions, and by professional doctors, particularly when considering the alternatives methods. Others were against it on grounds of human rights. The World Health Organisation has now also endorsed this view, claiming that:

> *the medicalisation of the procedure does not eliminate this harm and is inappropriate for two major reasons: genital mutilation runs against basic ethics of health care whereby unnecessary bodily mutilation cannot be condoned by health providers; and, its medicalisation seems to legitimise the harmful practice*
>
> WHO, 1997

With increasing pressure from FORWARD and other NGOs, the government passed the Prohibition of Female Circumcision Act (1985) preventing health professionals from carrying out these procedures. Section 1 (1) of the Act stated that subject to section 2 of the Act, it shall be an offence for any person:

a) to excise, inifibulate or otherwise mutilate the whole or any part of the labia majora or labia minora or clitoris of another person; or

b) to aid, alert, counsel or procure the performance by another person of any of those acts on that other person's own body.

The consequent penalties are:

c) on conviction or indictment, to a fine or to imprisonment for a term not exceeding five years or to both; or

d) on summary conviction, to a fine not exceeding the statutory maximum (as defined in section 74 of the Criminal Justice Act 1982) or to imprisonment for a term not exceeding six months, or to both.

The law therefore made it illegal for re-infibulation to be carried out following childbirth. The only discretion in the Act was provided by Section 2, which stated that the Act does not render unlawful a surgical operation necessary for the physical or mental health of a person on whom it is performed. This was probably intended to make permissible surgical procedures for gender reassignment, cosmetic surgery, and surgery for individuals suffering from body dysmorphia which, arguably, constitutes appropriate mental health grounds. Although there has been no clarification of what constitutes mental health grounds, the Act does state that no account is taken of any cultural beliefs, traditions or rituals which demand the practice.

As can be expected, though, some FGM-practising communities living in Britain have held onto their cultural beliefs, and have continued with the practice either illegally in this country or abroad, since the Act does not prohibit children from being taken out of the country to be circumcised. Clearly, the family's desire to stick to their cultural traditions and norms is sufficient moral ground for the continuation of the practice.

However, continued lobbying by NGOs highlighting FGM as a violation of a child's basic human rights also resulted in its being incorporated as a special case for concern in *Working Together under the Children's Act 1989: A Guide for Arrangements for Interagency Co-operation for the Protection of Children from Abuse*. These guidelines, issued by the Department of Health, advised workers to be alert to the issue of FGM within certain minority ethnic groups.

Further measures came in 1991, when core funding was granted by the Department of Health to FORWARD to help raise awareness and eradicate the practice of FGM. Later that same year, a survey was carried out by FORWARD which indicated a higher incidence of FGM than had previously been predicated. Consequently, a new updated guideline *Child Protection and FGM: Advice for Health, Education and Social Work Professionals* (Hedley and Dorkenoo, 1992), was issued to professionals outlining a framework for preventive action. This took into account the 1985 Act, the recommendations from *Working Together Under the Children's Act 1985,* as well as recommendations from African human rights experts and community leaders. It emphasised the need for professionals to support families through provision of education, awareness raising and counselling, whilst emphasising that a child should only be removed from the home as a last resort. This document also pushed for training and awareness raising for health and related professionals, and interagency co-operation, with social services acting as the lead agency.

As a member of the UN, the UK has also ratified and signed up to a number of UN Conventions. These include the UN Convention to eliminate all forms of Discrimination Against Women (CEDAW, 1979) and the UN Convention on the Rights of the Child (CRC, 1989). As a result, the UK is requested to monitor the implementation of the provision of such conventions via delegated ministerial groups.

In 1997, the Women's National Commission (WNC), an advisory committee to the government, expressed a number of concerns about girls at risk of FGM in the UK which were outlined in the document *Growing up female in the UK*, (1997). This included concerns not only about ineffective monitoring procedures to identify girls 'at risk' of being circumcised in the UK or abroad, but also about the inadequate protection available to this population. In addition, the commission commented on the absence of support for already circumcised women and girls who might be suffering physical or emotional problems secondary to circumcision. The WNC proposed a number of recommendations in the areas of social services, health and education calling for more proactive moves to help raise awareness about FGM and provide guidelines to professionals,

In 1998, further concerns around slow progress on the issue of FGM led FORWARD to commission another survey to determine firstly, whether statutory agencies were fulfilling their obligations under the 1985 Female Circumcision Act and the 1989 Children's Act, and secondly, whether the UK government was fulfilling its obligation to implement provisions in accordance with the international conventions. All local authorities (LAs) in England and Wales were sent questionnaires relating to inter-agency child protection procedures and interventions around FGM. The findings, which were published in the document *Out of Sight, Out of Mind* (1998), indicated that very little was going on. Few authorities had accurate data on the size of the population practising FGM in their area. More than half of LAs had no policy or procedure in place specifically relating to FGM. Contrary to anecdotal evidence indicating FGM to be occurring within certain communities, referrals of actual or suspected cases of FGM were low. These inadequate monitoring systems, allowed people to adopt a 'no problem here' attitude. Findings also highlighted the lack of training material available, both for professionals likely to encounter FGM, as well as for the communities practising it. On this basis, recommendations were made for more funding to be made available for these purposes, and guidelines were issued highlighting the steps that should be taken around child protection procedures.

Concerns around a lack of progress on education, prevention and prosecution were also debated by Peers in November 1998, after the issue of FGM was raised in the House of Lords by Baroness Gould. In 1999, the Department of Health (DoH) in conjunction with the Home Office (HO), and the then Department for Education and Employment (DfEE), issued joint guidelines in *Working Together to Safeguard Children – A Guide to Interagency Working to Safeguard and Promote the Welfare of Children*, (1999).These were disseminated to local authorities, health authorities, the police, probation, educational establishments, doctors, and a wide range of voluntary organisations working in the childcare field. Whilst this highlighted steps that should be taken to initiate child protection procedures where a child is felt to be at risk of FGM, there was little specific guidance other than giving local authorities the power to make enquiries and establish whether action was needed.

On 23 March 2000, the Parliamentary Under Secretary of State for the Department of Health, Lord Hunt of Kings Heath, said in the House of Lords:

> *education is central to eradicating the brutal practice of FGM. My department continues to fund relevant voluntary organisations. In addition, the government will ensure that the findings of the All Party Parliamentary Group (APPG) on population development and reproductive health on FGM are fed into the development of a clear sexual health strategy*
>
> Hunt, 2000

The findings of the APPG referred to above were published in November 2000, and were based on a questionnaire sent out to LAs, medical practitioners, refugee organisations, community workers, the UN and WHO and other leading organisations, both in the UK and abroad. A number of recommendations were proposed on the basis of its findings, which included repeated concerns over the absence of reliable, valid and up-to-date prevalence data on FGM in the UK. Other concerns noted were the lack of prosecutions to date, responsibility for education and strategies for social change being left largely to under-funded and poorly resourced NGOs, and a failure of the UK *Sex and Relationship Education Guidance* (DfEE 2000), to acknowledge FGM – contrary to the commitment expressed in 2000 by Lord Hunt. In addition, whilst protocols, guidelines and strategies were developed for medical professionals such as nurses, midwives, obstetricians and gynaecologists and Area Child Protection Committees (see section on Professional Guidelines), these were not widely disseminated. Similarly, the survey commissioned by FORWARD and funded by the Department of Health, which resulted in various recommendations made in the *Out of Sight Out of Mind* (1998) report, were not acted upon by the Department of Health. Against this background, the APPG made 28 separate recommendations covering legislation, education, community organisations, health and research.

Initiatives by professional bodies

A number of professional bodies have published guidelines or position papers on the issue of FGM. In 1983, the General Medical Council ruled that the performance of such an operation in the UK was unethical, and doctors could therefore be struck off the medical register for gross misconduct if found to be carrying out FGM. Both the Royal College of Obstetricians and Gynaecologists (RCOG) and the Royal College of Midwives (RCM) clarified their situation with regards to re-infibulation in light of the legislation on FGM, interpreting the law as permitting the reparation of the perineum or vulva if torn or being cut to facilitate delivery, but not to a degree that makes intercourse difficult or impossible (RCOG, 1997; RCM, 1998). The RCOG has recently reissued its statement on FGM (RCOG, 2003).

In 1998, the Royal College of Midwives (RCM) issued a position paper on FGM (RCM, 1998) outlining guidelines specifying the role of the midwife not only with regards to the practice around de-infibulation, but also within the context of child protection and working with families on issues relating to FGM. In March 1994, guidance was issued by the Royal College of Nursing (RCN) to raise awareness and understanding amongst nurses to stimulate discussion about local service responses to FGM, and these were re-issued in October 1996. British Medical Association (BMA) guidelines were issued in 1996 (and re-issued in 2001), emphasising the need to raise awareness of the health and legal issues around FGM, and the need to disseminate information to professionals as well as communities about the services and sources of information available. UNICEF and other agencies of the United Nations have also called for refugee and asylum status to be granted to women and girls fleeing their country to escape genital mutilation.

The BMA supported this, and in 1997, issued guidelines on *Access to Healthcare for Asylum Seekers*, (1997), outlining the health care rights of asylum seekers arriving in the UK. Area Child Protection Committees (ACPCs) have a responsibility for developing inter-agency policies and procedures for child protection as well as a duty to scrutinise inter-agency training and make recommendations accordingly. Guidelines were issued by the Department of Health in

Working Together to Safeguard Children: A Guide to Inter-Agency Working to Safeguard and Promote the Welfare of Children, (1997), advising local agencies to be alert to the possibility of FGM occurring in their locality, amongst certain minority ethnic communities. It also recommended that preventive strategies be introduced in areas where there were affected communities.

At present whilst some of the professional bodies have developed training manuals and guidelines on FGM, these are not mandatory upon their staff and members. This is a serious failing in light of the fact that illiteracy and ignorance of FGM can lead to the mismanagement of cases, precipitating physical and psychological distress for women (Lockhat, 1999).

Initiatives by NGOs

Very few charities and NGOs are working at the grass roots level in the area of FGM in the UK. Those that are, tend to have limited funding and resources available. Some of the more active and involved ones include the following:

The Foundation for Women's Health Research and Development (FORWARD) is the most active organisation working in the area of FGM. It was established in 1983 by Efua Dorkenoo, OBE, as an independent organisation to take forward recommendations made by the Minority Rights Group, which included raising the issue of FGM and seeing it recognised as a human rights issue. In 1985 FORWARD became a registered charity and, two decades later, it is now a firmly established and growing NGO dedicated to serving the health and human rights needs of African women both in Africa and the UK. It provides education and support to communities, information and advice to professionals within health, education, social services and other statutory organisations, undertakes research, and works at both national and international levels. Since 1984, it has received core funding on an annual basis from the Department of Health.

The Black Women's Health and Family Support (BWHFS), formerly the London Black Women's Health Action Project (LBWHAP), was founded in 1982 to address the health needs of black women (and particularly Somali women) in London. Jointly funded by the London Borough of Tower Hamlets, and the London Boroughs Grants Committee, BWHFS has campaigned against FGM through adopting a holistic approach which has included running workshops for communities and professionals, doing outreach and development work, and providing advocacy services for Somali women. One of the main aims of grassroots work has been to change attitudes and explain the religious stance on the issue and to get people to think about why they continue with the practice.

The Research, Action and Information Network for the Bodily Integrity of Women (Rainbo) is an international not-for-profit organisation working on issues that intersect between women's health and human rights. Work is focused on programmes in Africa and with African immigrant and refugee communities.

Local responses and initiatives

In addition to the efforts of NGOs, there are many religious and community figures from both practising and non-practising communities, who are striving to stamp out the practice of FGM with the help of local initiatives and community organisations. For example, El Hadj O Barud, a local Somali religious leader based in Manchester, has openly argued that:

> *it* (FGM) *is a child abuse*

WHO, 1999

Others, like Professor Abdel Haleem, Director, Centre for Islamic Studies, SOAS, University of London has pointed out that:

> *this mutilation is obviously harmful and anything which is harmful is forbidden in Islam. It is not mentioned in the Qur'an, our most sacred text*

WHO, 1999

Moreover, in October 2002, for the second year running, FORWARD was invited by the Islamic Cultural Centre and the Central Mosque in Regent's Park, London, to participate in a health fair to raise awareness about the issue of FGM, which attracted over 1,300 people.

Clearly, such responses coupled with positive local initiatives are having an effect. There are many more men now who are beginning to speak out against the practice. However, most of the positive local initiatives tend to have a short life span because of the short-term nature of funding. As a result, sustainable development and progress has not been possible. Those short-term positive local initiatives that have had some success have included the following:

Kensington, Chelsea and Westminster (KCW) Health Authority funded a project in conjunction with the Sudanese community in West London. A video launched in February 1999 entitled *It's for us to decide, (1999),* made in conjunction with local schools, and men, women and community leaders from the Sudanese community. The video (recorded in Arabic with English subtitles) tells the story of a young recently married couple experiencing problems with consummation because of infibulation. It illustrates their struggle to cope with pressures from their families, as they take the decision to have the circumcision undone. The video was made for awareness raising within local Sudanese communities, and also as a training tool for professionals to facilitate their understanding of the cultural context around FGM. KCW health authority also gave FORWARD a six month grant to carry out a survey in the borough, looking at the knowledge, attitude and practices of FGM amongst the Somali, Ethiopian, Sudanese and Eritrean communities settled in the area, and professionals working with them. The study revealed 81 per cent of women of childbearing age, as having been circumcised – thus highlighting the need for health professionals to be engaged with the issue.

The Midlands Refugee Council FGM Project was a three-year project funded by the National Lottery Charities Board in 1997. The aim of the project was to help eradicate FGM through the provision of information, advice and guidelines for men and women amongst Sudanese, Somali, and Yemeni refugee communities, and raising awareness amongst social workers, teachers, and health professionals.

The Haween Support Group, part of the Women's Rights Group (a sub-group of the Manchester Child Protection Committee), is a local community organisation for Somali women in Manchester. It looks to improve the quality of life for the Somali community by addressing the wider community issues, and encouraging engagement with voluntary and statutory bodies to effect change. A successful bid was made to the Global Development fund, which led to the setting up of the Somali Women in the Community (SWITCH) project from January – April 1999, which provided a series of workshops for Somali women around health issues and in particular FGM.

The joint funded project by FORWARD sponsored by Comic Relief and the Department of Health, involved carrying out small-scale awareness and training needs assessments amongst professionals working in the London Borough of Hounslow, Cardiff, Birmingham, Liverpool, Manchester and Bristol. In response to the findings, FORWARD conducted interagency training for health, education, social services and the police to address the gaps.

De-infibulation clinics. There are now a number of NHS funded

African well-women clinics set up and run in various parts of London as well as other parts of the country, such as Liverpool and Birmingham. The clinics offer free de-infibulation services and general advice to those who have undergone FGM. Services are confidential and run by staff fully trained in the area of FGM.

Real commitment or 'lip service'?

Over the last two decades, it can be seen how debates around FGM have dipped in and out of the limelight, dictated by media interest, political agendas, events, and campaigning organisations.

What is clearly apparent is that things have barely moved on. Recommendations made in the late 1980s bear uncomfortable similarities to those being made today. There is still no effective procedure in place either to identify girls 'at risk' or to identify those that have been taken abroad to be circumcised. There is no effective training, information or guidance for health providers and professionals. Although some professional bodies do have guidelines about how to deal with FGM, these vary in quality, but more importantly, they are not mandatory for any professional body at present. There are currently very few support systems available for girls who have been circumcised and who may be in need of help. Whilst several FGM working groups have been set up in some parts of the country by professionals and groups interested in the issue, there is currently no co-ordinated approach or national strategy led by the government to deal with the issue. This has been raised again and again as a point of concern, and most recently in March 2003:

> The NHS has very little data about FGM, largely because it has not set out to look for such data. Our report (APPG Population development and reproductive Health 2000) recommended that the Department of Health should undertake much more data collection and then make use of those data when developing policies. So far, that has not happened. I am aware that the specialist NGO, FORWARD, has applied to the Department of Health for project grants to collect data on FGM and to address linked practices. I believe that FORWARD and similar groups are especially well placed to do that work. I have written to the Secretary of State to reiterate the need to obtain accurate data on the prevalence of FGM in the UK as soon as possible
>
> McCafferty, 2003

All the evidence seems to indicate that commitment to the issue of FGM is very much at a 'lip service' level. Recommendations on FGM by working groups set up and fully endorsed by the government, have all too often failed to be taken forward and acted upon. This is not only a waste of resources, but also a betrayal of the trust and confidence of community workers and communities themselves, who are very often reluctant to talk about the issue, but do so when told their contributions will make a difference and help their communities. Similarly, as mentioned earlier, many of the positive initiatives that have been carried out at local level with communities have had to rely on short-term funding initiatives, which is once again frustrating to communities and undermines their confidence. Adwoa Kwateng-Kluvitse, director of FORWARD, makes the point:

> *I think they* (the government) *need to look at the reality of funding projects for FGM. It's not only the amount but also the length of time that's important. If they are committed as was stated in the APPG, they need to put their money where their mouth is*
>
> Kwateng-Kluvitse, 2003

She goes further to give an example relating to the absence of prevalence data in this country:

> *FORWARD has asked for research money to operationalise this action, which has been a recommendation since the 1980s*

It is widely acknowledged that the illegality of the practice means researchers and activists often meet a wall of silence when attempting to tackle the issues with communities, and that this makes it a difficult issue to address. People who practise FGM tend to live in close-knit communities often holding steadfast to their traditions and community values. Most are unlikely to 'betray' each other to the law. Many of the victims are so young and vulnerable, and know their parents love them and want to do what is best for them. Furthermore, they are brought up to respect the decisions of their parents, so much so that offences are not likely to be reported. Similarly, whilst professionals may be aware that the practice may be going on, not having the right tools and training may hinder them from taking a stance and, as a result, referrals of actual or suspected cases of circumcision to child protection agencies may be low.

To date, only two doctors have been struck off after having been found guilty of serious professional misconduct before the General Medical Council. In the first of these in 1993, the doctor was struck off the medical register for performing FGM while knowing that it was illegal. The police, however, refused to prosecute. In 2000, another doctor was struck off for offering to carry out the practice.

In view of the above, it is ironic that of the 28 recommendations made by the APPG in 2000 (spanning health, education, training, voluntary organisations, research, and legislation), the only ones that have been acted upon to date, are those concerning legislation, as will be discussed in the next section.

The new FGM legislation

In March 2003 a private bill was proposed to parliament recommending a number of amendments to the Prohibition of Female Circumcision Act 1985 including:

➡ Prosecution of a person who has aided, abetted, counselled, procured, excised, infibulated a girl/woman abroad, despite FGM being legal in the country where it was performed.

➡ Conviction of indictment to be lengthened to between four and ten years.

➡ Changing title of the 1985 Act from Prohibition of Female Circumcision Act to Prohibition of Female Genital Mutilation.

This has been welcomed by many working to eradicate the practice, since a high proportion of parents take their daughters abroad to be circumcised. As Dr Khaled, a Sudanese Gynaecologist based in Manchester, explained:

> *because of the regulation they don't do it here but they go on holiday, they do it at home, and they come back...*(it's) *because of the family pressure*
>
> WHO, 1999

Others, however, are sceptical in view of the fact that there have been no prosecutions to date under the current legislation. It poses the question as to whether tightening the law in the absence of any other proactive action to work with communities will have any effect or will, in fact, push the practice further underground. This does need careful consideration, particularly when bearing in mind the findings of a recent 1998 survey commissioned by the Department of Health which looked at the experiences, attitudes and beliefs of young single Somalis living in London. A substantial proportion of both males (42 per cent) and females (18 per cent) reported that they intended to circumcise their own daughters and would not be deterred by legislation (DoH, 1998).

Moreover, Dr Khaled carried out a survey in Manchester, which showed that:

> *80 per cent said that they would continue* (with the practice)
> *because of the family pressure*
>
> WHO, 1999

Ultimately then, the move to tighten the law is more than likely to have a more detrimental effect on women and girls themselves, making them more reluctant to come forward for help and support for fear of repercussions to their family. The other key point, which the legislation fails to take into account, is that decisions are not necessarily made by parents *themselves*. As I have shown elsewhere (Lockhat, H 1999), in 16 per cent of cases, either one, or both parents were against having their daughters circumcised, but this was nevertheless overridden by the elders of the family. The legislation therefore takes a very 'white eurocentric' perspective on family decision-making processes, and parental responsibility.

Concerns about the uni-dimensional focus on the law were expressed by some MPs at the second reading of the Bill in March 2003:

> *It is important to note what is not covered by the Bill. It does not require health professionals and other relevant authorities to report incidences of FGM. It does not touch on Department of Health issues such as ensuring that all medical personnel are trained in cultural sensitivity and how to meet the needs of women who have undergone FGM. It does not cover the practicalities and difficulties in social services taking action under the Children Act 1989 or child protection procedures, which I know is a big issue. I mention all those areas because they were raised in the recommendations made by the All-Party Group in its report of November 2000*
>
> Gillan, 2003

> *Not only should FGM be made illegal and educational programmes be initiated, but social workers and the medical professions should be included in the fight to eliminate the practice. Their participation is crucial. The British Medical Association has published detailed guidelines on FGM that are of interest to many of those who must deal with women who suffer the after-effects of FGM. That demonstrates the influence that doctors, nurses, social workers and teachers can have when they work in communities that practice FGM. Their sensitive involvement can have a lasting effect, particularly among younger women*
>
> Roe, 2003

Such views are also shared by FORWARD. Kwateng-Kluvitse feels that the tightening of the law must be backed by holistic programmes and initiatives, including what she calls a 'cross-generational empowerment' programme. She argues that:

> *It's not enough to take a reactive approach. As part of a preventive, proactive approach, we need not only to be educating adult females to not circumcise their daughters, but also to be empowering young girls specifically, to be able to speak out*
>
> Kwateng-Kluvitse, 2003

For Kwateng-Kluvitse this could easily happen if the DfES includes an FGM module, where appropriate, into the personal, health, and social education (PHSE) syllabus for schools to follow. Other community activists like Mohamed in Manchester suggest that:

> *there should be a national standardised booklet* (by the DfES) *on the legislation and health consequences, which nursery schools could issue to parents where relevant*
>
> Mohamed, 2003

This would be a proactive measure targeting parents at a crucial early stage. There should also be a clear unequivocal commitment to eradicating or drastically reducing the prevalence of the practice within a defined time frame:

> *all it takes is one generation to stop doing it and the cycle could be broken...they* (the government) *should, therefore, clearly identify a year by which it aims to abolish FGM* (in the UK)
>
> Kwateng-Kluvitse, 2003

However, these views seem to be falling on deaf ears. As the government presses ahead with the new legislation, it is sending out the message that legislation is the priority. For those like Kwateng-Kluvitse, the government has taken the easy option by 'focusing on the recommendation (APPG) that has cost nothing', rather than adopting a national holistic programme of action.

CHAPTER SEVEN

WOMEN'S PHYSICAL EXPERIENCES

Introduction

Female circumcision is associated with a high incidence of complications – immediate and long-term, physical, sexual and psychological, ranging from minor, to severe and even fatal cases. Techniques of FGM vary across communities, according to cultural and folklore background. Complications arising will be largely dependent on the type of FGM carried out, methods used to carry it out, and the skill of the operator.

Whilst there are many studies documenting the physical effects of FGM and the difficulties that can arise throughout life, most of these have been carried out in countries where FGM is common practice, and difficulties arising are more to do with lack of resources. In western countries, such as the UK, although resources are available or could quite easily be made available to meet the health and social care needs of circumcised women, it is more often the lack of understanding and consequent lack of preparedness, in addition to the attitudes of many professionals towards the issue, that lead to devastating consequences for the health and well-being of these women.

This, and the following two chapters, are based on a qualitative study carried out in the urban areas of south Manchester with women from Sudanese and Somali communities looking at their experiences, perceptions, and views of FGM (Lockhat, 1999). It is a powerful recording of the accounts of many women. Whilst chapter eight deals with their psychological experiences and chapter nine with their experiences of the health and social care services, the present chapter documents their experiences of the physical problems encountered throughout their lives. For many women, the most difficult physical problems experienced coincide with various lifecycle events, such as immediately post-circumcision, at menstruation, at the time of marriage, and during childbirth. The quotes used in this chapter are as spoken by the women themselves.

Physical complications

It is a widely held finding that the 'mild' form of circumcision (where the clitoris is conserved) inflicts the least physical damage, and is associated with fewest physical complications. It is the more severe excision and infibulation-type operations that can lead to complications which are usually classified as immediate or delayed.

My study showed that mildly circumcised women did not report any significant physical or psychological complications secondary to their circumcision, whilst most women who had been infibulated recalled subsequent physical or medical complications at various life cycle stages (Lockhat, 1999). The following, therefore, is a brief summary outlining common physical sequelae to infibulation-type circumcision, and incorporates the experiences of the women.

I   Immediate complications

Immediate complications include bleeding, wound infection, pain, urinary complications, and trauma to adjacent tissue and, in extreme cases, even death.

Mortality

In light of the clandestine nature of the operation, fatalities do occur, arising more often from haemorrhage or septicaemia, but tending to be attributed to other causes such as evil spirits or God's will.

Pain

The clitoris and labia are amongst the most sensitive areas of the body, and in the absence of anaesthetic, pain is severe and the main cause of shock. Although the pain tends to subside over time, infection to the raw area of the wound can lead to intense pain and restricted movement. Some women described the pain as follows:

> *I had to lie down because I couldn't walk. So I stayed in that position for five days... and afterwards* (after the operation) *after a few hours, when the ladies had gone and when the anaesthetic had worn off, I felt all the pain...*
>
> participant 35

> *I could only lie on my back, couldn't turn. I got up seven or eight days later...*
>
> participant 44

felt too much pain... I cried and screamed. I had to lie down for one week, and would wake up in a lot of pain. Had great difficulty...

participant 53

I had to stay three months at home because I was weak and I couldn't physically move...

participant 19

Bleeding

Bleeding is unavoidable in operations of this nature but is controllable if sufficient pressure is applied. Occasionally, however, severance to the clitoral artery can lead to severe bleeding with great risk to life in the absence of a blood transfusion or surgical intervention.

As some women recollected:

on the eighth day, I woke up early morning, and felt the bed was all wet and I saw blood everywhere. My mum didn't talk to my dad but called my aunt and they took me to see a specialist doctor. I remember when he took me to the other room and told me I had a fever, and he had to do an operation to stop the bleeding. All I remember is he started pressing, and his shirt was covered in blood. I was then taken home and had to stay in bed for two days... and I vaguely remember I had to go back to have the stitches removed...

participant 14

my aunt and grandma put their hands on my legs and my grandma said 'do a perfect pharaonic one' and the lady started. The lady cut deep in the vein, I saw blood...

participant 12

Infection

Fatal cases of tetanus have been recorded following such operations (Shandall 1967). Unsterilised equipment can give rise to infection as can bandaging the legs together after the operation, which can prevent adequate draining of the wound and lead to ascending infections to the vagina, cervix and uterus (Modawi 1974). Use of thorns in place of stitches can also give rise to infection and interfere with healing.

As some women recalled:

after seven days the woman came to remove thorns. She missed one, which got infected and led to fever and illness. Had to go to doctor, who found and removed it...

participant 45

for me it took four checks to heal and each time she (circumcisor)
*would have to put new thorns in and it was very painful all over
again...*

participant 44

Urinary complications

Urinary retention is a common sequelae within forty-eight hours of the
operation and usually results from intense pain. A number of women
had vivid recollections of the problems they experienced the first time
they needed to void urine:

*I held my urine in for days and when I passed it was like having
the cutting done over again...*

participant 44

*I was advised to urinate twenty minutes after, but I had to stop
because of the pain, although my sister managed to go, and she
felt better than me. I retained for one day and had a fever the next
day. My mum tried to force me to go by telling me that if I didn't
she would call the midwife again...*

participant 19

*it was very painful. I had stitches and had to lie and rest for five
days and had problems going to the toilet. I used to hold my urine
in and my stomach became big, and I was crying because I
wanted to have an operation to pass the urine out...*

participant 36

*the worst thing was the wee, I'll never forget the pain. I held it for
three days so that when I did wee, it broke a stitch. No one can
imagine the pain...*

participant 26

*very difficult at first. It's kind of similar to after you have had
stitches after childbirth but as a child you are less prepared for
these problems...*

participant 15

*at night I felt hurting in that area. I could not pass urine. I was
crying, and felt physically unwell because of my full bladder. I had
like a coma because of this...*

participant 19

Difficulties also arise due to the tightness of the closure:

*I didn't wee for two days because it was so painful. Eventually
they had to open it a little because I couldn't go, so I had two
holes...*

participant 53

Infection can also lead to inadequate healing of the wound edges, such that the flow of urine is not from a single orifice, but drains in several places.

Damage to other tissue

Trauma to adjacent tissue such as the urethra, anus and vagina, has been recorded and can arise from a struggling child, primitive instruments, or a clumsy inexperienced operator (Hathout, 1963).

II Delayed complications

Delayed complications of infibulation-type circumcision include menstrual, coital, and obstetric difficulties.

Urinary complications

Past studies in Sudan by El Dareer (1983b) and in Somalia by Brown et al (1989), have found urinary disturbances to be the most common ongoing complication – particularly recurrent urinary tract infection. Difficulties urinating can persist for many years after infibulation-type operations, due to the bridge, which forms in front of the vaginal entrance, distorting the urinary stream, and leading to constant saturation of this skin.

Menstrual problems

Menstrual blood, unable to drain because of the restricted opening, can lead to haematocolpos – the accumulation of blood in the vagina. This usually presents as increasing abdominal distension and monthly discomfort without bleeding. More common, however, is the incidence of dysmenorrhoea (painful periods).

Over half of the infibulated women in my study had experienced this.

> *severe pain and vomiting each time had period... had to take painkillers this improved when it* (circumcision scar) *was opened...*
>
> participant 50

> *very little blood could escape...also very painful periods. Still have problems now...*
>
> participant 16

> *used to have very painful periods ...it was like having a baby I would vomit and it was just so painful... but this stopped when I got married...*
>
> participant 26

I always had very painful periods...not sure if this was related to the circumcision. At one point I went to the doctors and they said they would open the hole a bit, because it was very small. I was engaged and refused to have this done because it is shameful...

participant 27

I used to have a lot of pain for the first few days, and used to get blood clots, which I had to dislodge with my fingers. It used to smell too...

participant 38

problems with the flow of blood, and used to get a lot of pain...

participant 31

Calculus

Tight scars can lead to calcification arising from incomplete drainage of menstrual and urinary deposits. Over time this can lead to the formation of calculi – hardened deposits.

Cysts

Dermoid cysts are a frequently cited complication of circumcision. The cysts vary in size, and on occasion become infected and present as very painful abscesses.

Infection

Pelvic infections have been reported and can potentially affect fertility, and lead to chronic morbidity.

Ulcer

Urine retention can lead to the formation of painful ulcers underneath the infibulated area of the vulva. Partial de-infibulation may be required to treat this in order for topical applications to be applied.

Keloid scars

Dark skin has been associated with an increased tendency to form keloidal scars, which in some cases can be large enough to interfere with ease of intercourse or delivery. Some women can feel quite distressed by these growths, which can sometimes be treated by surgical excision and steroidal treatments, though in some cases, more specialised techniques such as radiation are necessary.

Catheterisation

FGM scars can impede the insertion of catheters, which may be necessary during surgical operations or in cases where there is a need to monitor urinary output.

HIV

Although there is no evidence of a link between FGM and Human Immunodeficiency Virus (HIV), more recently and particularly in the poorer nations, concern has arisen about the high risk of HIV transmission through the use of non-sterilised instruments for multiple operations.

III Coital difficulties

Additional common problems for this population group – though rarely reported because of cultural taboos, are coital difficulties.

Sensitivity

Heightened sensitivity and tenderness to the vulva area, perineum and vagina can lead to painful intercourse and delivery. Psychological factors, such as anxiety, are also possible contributing factors that cannot be ruled out. Management options to deal with such complaints should they arise, should include possible referrals to psychological or counselling services, where techniques such as desensitisation may prove useful.

Restricted entry

Restricted entry means that penetration is not possible without pain and discomfort unless the circumcision scar is opened (de-infibulated). In some parts of Somalia, it is standard practice for the midwife to visit a woman in the few days prior to marriage to open the circumcision scar slightly, to facilitate penetration. In the UK, however, whilst there are African well-women clinics now available in *some* parts of the country, women are not always able to have this done, either because they are not aware of these clinics, or have difficulty accessing them.

This was the experience of one woman:

> *in the UK, this* (de-infibulation) *is something done within the community because of the lack of services for such procedures...*
> participant 55

In cases where de-infibulation does not occur prior to consummation, husbands often force themselves through or they (husband or someone from community) attempt to enlarge the hole with their fingernails, razors or some other sharp instrument.

As one woman from the study reported:

> *when I got married I was in this country so there were no doctors I knew to de-infibulate me so a woman* (from the community) *just*

came and cut me with no anaesthetic and I had to have sex straight after... it was very painful... the pain lasted three weeks...

participant 35

Dyspareunia

Dyspareunia (painful intercourse) is a very common difficulty and can result from painful memories of the process of circumcision, painful circumcision scars or diminished vaginal secretion (Mahran, 1981).

Over three quarters of infibulated women in my study cited problems during their first intercourse:

for the first time, it was very difficult, and for two to three weeks after the pain of intercourse was bad. There was no enjoyment for me and that put me off, and I would try to stay away...

participant 19

I had problems for the first two weeks. I was opened the second day after marriage. On the first night my husband tried and it was very painful, very difficult. It was still difficult after opening...

participant 27

A quarter of the women reported having current sexual problems ranging from diminished desire for sex:

it's not that enjoyable now. Sometimes I don't feel interested but I haven't ever avoided...

participant 2

I always feel cheated out of more sexual pleasure. After my first child, I lost my sex drive for quite a while. But this time after my second child, I have lost it completely...

participant 15

to avoidance of it completely:

it got a little better with time but I avoided sex whenever I could...

participant 16

I have refused to do it completely...

participant 55

Sexual dysfunction

Diminished desire or indifference towards intercourse can often result because of the accompanying difficulties described above. In addition, other sexually related problems including dyspareunia, apareunia and vaginismus can present.

This was the experience of one woman in the study, whose difficulties may have been secondary to circumcision:

> *I have suffered from vaginal itching for which I've had to have medication. It's made sex very painful...*
>
> participant 14

Anal intercourse

Difficulties with vaginal penetration can lead to anal intercourse. This method of intercourse is not free from complication, but can lead to tissue damage and distortion to the anal passage, which can cause incontinence.

Male sexual dysfunction

FGM can also have repercussions on male sexuality, as indicated by some studies, which show a link between dyspareunia and vaginismus, and impotence and premature ejaculation (Mahran, 1981).

IV Obstetric complications

Obstetric complications commonly reported are largely the result of restricted openings, which interfere with examination and delivery.

Internal examination

Tight, unopened circumcision scars and heightened sensitivity to the vaginal and vulval areas, can make internal examinations antenatally and/or during labour very painful. Tight unopened circumcision scars can further complicate such examinations making it difficult to detect fibroids and ectopic pregnancy.

Delivery problems

Where de-infibulation has not occurred prior to delivery, difficulties can arise with undertaking examinations during labour, including the inability to accurately monitor the foetus. Prolonged labour can lead to tearing of the scar causing excruciating pain as well as bleeding and injury to adjacent structures such as the urethra, and perineal laceration. Extreme cases of obstructed labour can also lead to foetal distress precipitating brain damage or even mortality.

Of the women who had had children, over two thirds reported experiencing delivery complications. Some of these had given birth in their own countries where procedures for delivery with respect to FGM are familiar but nevertheless difficult:

> *at delivery had to make a cut and sew again. After that you spend days and days until it heals and it's very painful...*
>
> participant 1

and often complicated because of a severe lack of resources:

> *first baby was very difficult, and I was very ill afterwards... there were no doctors or nurses because of the war... I thought I would die...*
>
> participant 48

Women who gave birth in the UK felt that their difficulties were the result of the incompetent actions of the physicians, driven by a lack of understanding of how to manage such deliveries:

> *with the first child, the doctors didn't know how to deal with me and had to call a Nigerian doctor...*
>
> participant 9

or inappropriate procedures carried out:

> *although the doctors here didn't know much about circumcision, I was lucky because my first baby was quite small. My second child was a big baby so they cut everywhere and I suffered a lot after...*
>
> participant 35

> *the first child was very difficult because of the way they cut me. For twelve days I couldn't even sit. I couldn't feed the baby and things remained difficult after the birth... I felt very sick after and couldn't even look after my child...*
>
> participant 5

> *this was another nightmare. They cut me up and down and the sides...*
>
> participant 44

Infertility

Infections ascending up the genital tract as a result of FGM may render females infertile.

This was possibly the case with one woman in my study:

> *I have not been able to conceive, but not sure if this is related to circumcision...*
>
> participant 46

In many FGM-practising communities, there is a high status associated with childbearing. The stigma attached to not being able to have children, therefore, can have both social and psychological repercussions.

Healing

Existing scar tissue from the time of circumcision may mean that tears during childbirth may take longer to heal and be more susceptible to infection, due to the reduced blood supply to these areas. If not treated, postpartum infection to wounds can lead to puerperal sepsis.

As one woman recollected:

healing of stitching afterwards caused discomfort...

participant 36

CHAPTER EIGHT

WOMEN'S PSYCHOLOGICAL EXPERIENCES

Introduction

This chapter focuses on women's psychological experiences. Whilst numerous studies have been done to assess the potential physical impact of FGM, far less has been done in regard to psychological and emotional consequences. In a recent review of the literature looking at the mental health consequences of circumcision, 504 articles were identified of which less than twenty contained primary data on the psychological sequelae (WHO, 1998b). This is due partly to difficulties in measuring psychological distress, and partly with the reluctance of women to discuss these issues. Thus, many assumptions have been made about likely effects of circumcision on women's psychological and emotional well-being. Most studies carried out to date have comprised case reports, case series, surveys, and interviews with health professionals.

Whilst there have been reports of phobic reactions, chronic irritability, fear of sexual relations, loss of self esteem, feelings of victimisation, severe anxiety prior to the operation, depression, and sexual frustration, there have also been contradictory findings indicating an absence of psychopathology (Burstyn, 1995; Toubia, 1994; Arbesman, Kahler and Buck, 1993; Lightfoot-Klein, 1989; Moen, 1983; Mahran, 1981; Basher, 1977; 1982; Verzin, 1977). An absence of concrete data, therefore, makes it difficult to provide mental health and social care services to help and support circumcised women, as there is uncertainty as to the type of support required, and the best way of providing this.

This chapter aims to fill this gap by shedding light on the kinds of psychological problems circumcised women living in the UK are experiencing. The first section of the chapter looks at women's subjective recollection of their circumcision experience, and discusses the nature of their psychological and emotional distress, the second section looks at prevalence rates of clinical psychopathology amongst the sample of women, and the final section addresses predictors in the development of clinical psychopathology.

I Subjective recollections

Women were asked to think back to the time when they were actually circumcised, and whether they could recall their parents' attitude towards the practice. Only very few were unable to remember any aspect of the event. Of the majority who did remember, most were able to give very vivid accounts, detailing the preparation beforehand, their feelings in anticipation of the event, details of where the operation was carried out, who was present, whether anaesthetic was used, how they felt during the operation, and what they remembered happening before and after in terms of ceremony and recovery. What was most interesting was their recollection of their parents' attitudes towards the ceremony. Whilst in most cases women recalled both parents having condoned the practice, in almost one fifth of cases, this was not the case. A few women recalled both parents being very much against it, but it was instigated by the grandmother:

> *my mum and dad didn't want it done... my aunt and grandma took me from my mum when my dad was out of town... my father was very angry and didn't speak to his mother for two months...*
>
> participant 12

> *my parents were very angry because it was my grandma who had it done... they were against it...*
>
> participant 52

Some remembered their mother arranging for it to be carried out against the wishes of their father, who in some cases, condemned it on the grounds that it was not an Islamic practice:

> *my dad was a sheikh and said it was not Islamic so he wouldn't do it... it was my mum who paid for it... When she did it my dad was upset and angry. He shouted at my mother and at the lady shouting 'we don't want it. We don't want our daughter circumcised'...*
>
> participant 35

> *my father was a sheikh... I remember he was not that happy...*
>
> participant 19

Others were merely opposed to the practice:

> *I remember my father was crying 'why did you do this?' and didn't speak to my mother for a month...*
>
> participant 17

> *my father was against it... It's the women who try to stop men talking against this...father didn't like to see me suffer and he was angry with my mum for this, cause they did it when he was not there...*
>
> participant 9

> *my dad was very angry about it and shouted at my mum...*
>
> participant 34

Preparation prior to the actual operation

Preparation prior to the event varied greatly from no preparation:

> *on the day, I was just woken up... my mother told me 'you are going to be circumcised...*
>
> participant 44

to extensive preparation sometimes weeks before the event:

> *it was a big occasion they prepared from a month before. Me and my sister* (were circumcised) *on the same day. Had new clothes and furniture, and painted the house. It was the first occasion in our house. Close relatives came to the house the night before.. extended family were invited to the celebrations which went on for three days ...*
>
> participant 4

Feelings before the operation

Feelings before the operation varied widely between participants. Many reported feeling very excited in anticipation:

> *you feel it's good when you see other kids being circumcised. We are happy although after circumcision, you do feel pain. I had seen my cousin circumcised and I wanted it. There was no presents, no party. The day of the circumcision they told me... I was happy...*
>
> participant 27

> *I was nine years old. My stepmother and all were there. I'd seen some other girls older than me have it done, so I wanted it done and I was happy to have it done...*
>
> participant 36

Others reported wanting to have it done, but not really knowing what it actually involved:

> *I remember, I pushed my mother to do it, because I saw my friends having it done… I didn't know what it was but I thought it sounded nice. But when it was done, it hurt…*
>
> participant 28

Some were indifferent:

> *As a child you see all the girls experience it. Maybe you put in your mind it's a normal thing…*
>
> participant 1

or did not know what was involved and yet felt fearful:

> *I didn't know what was going to happen. There was just fear…*
>
> participant 31

> *I didn't know what was going to happen before the operation, so I was happy because I thought it would be something good, and I was telling everyone I'd be having it done. Didn't realise what would happen…*
>
> participant 55

Others remembered past occasions where they had witnessed the circumcision of other girls and had recollections of the screaming, the pain, and the blood and knew what was going to happen and were very scared.

> *it was the day before my operation that my mother told me that tomorrow I would be circumcised. I knew what it meant…I was very frightened and I couldn't eat anything…*
>
> participant 38

> *I was scared of it before I had it. My mum had told me I said… 'don't like it. I'm scared don't like blood'. She started giving me money and said 'I'll buy gold for you… everyone will give you money'… I didn't care I was still scared…*
>
> participant 9

> *I was very anxious because some girls had died because of bleeding…*
>
> participant 37

and there were many reports of girls terrified, running and hiding from village elders:

> *I felt very, very scared, and tried to hide…*
>
> participant 44

Memories of the actual operation

Very few participants had no recollection whatsoever of the actual operation:

> I can't remember anything about the operation...
>
> participant 43

Most participants were able to describe the actual operation in great detail:

> she (the midwife) came about 6.30am... I remember because the sun was rising. I was taken to another room, a smaller room apart from the main building. The servants' room. There was my mother and three other women. They put me on a low stool and one woman held my shoulders, one my legs, and they were trying to hold me down. The operator started things... it was horrible, painful, I cried and shouted, and tried to run but I couldn't. The operation took forty-five minutes for the slicing and the stitching and I was not being still. I can remember my mum saying 'take out all the black skin, take it all out'...
>
> participant 38

> I remember it was about 5.30am, women came from East Sudan. One had a little knife in her pocket. Four big women had to hold me, my shoulders, my back and one held my legs...
>
> participant 20

Feelings during the operation

Whilst some women could not recall whether anaesthetic had been used or not, over one third reported being operated on without any anaesthetic, and all but two had been infibulated:

> for the actual operation there was an old woman. She wasn't a proper midwife, no medicine, no anaesthetic... They caught my arms and legs... it is all very stupid, I can remember the pain, I screamed... I screamed for three days...
>
> participant 9

> five women held our arms and legs and there was no injection (anaesthetic) and a lot of bleeding... I shaked a lot and I struggled. They called someone else to hold me... It was very very bad...
>
> participant 37

> No injection (anaesthetic) was given. I think I was in a chair. They held me down with their hands. I can remember when they cut me, I didn't scream or shout a lot, but I had a lot of pain... after

the circumcision I had a lot of pain, and shaking and bleeding. I had to rest to recover...

participant 27

In the absence of any anaesthetic, the pain experienced in an operation of this kind on such a sensitive part of the body is likely to be beyond comprehension. Many women could not describe in words how they had felt at this moment. Others reported feelings of complete helplessness:

the whole operation went through and I couldn't do anything...

participant 20

I didn't struggle because I was shocked it was happening...

participant 30

Feelings after the operation

Feelings after the operation were very wide ranging. Many reported feelings of great happiness simply because it was regarded as a normal procedure within the culture:

I felt happy afterwards because I thought everyone has it, it is common...

participant 28

it felt really painful but I didn't feel angry, I felt proud because all had had it done...

participant 33

For others, feelings ranged from indifference:

my attitude was it's been done, it's over. I have to get on with it...

participant 30

to sadness and confusion:

I didn't know it would be that bad because as a child and when little you cannot say anything. I can't describe my feelings...

participant 20

I had this sick feeling in my head, even as a teenager...

participant 55

I was really sad. I didn't know the implications then... but I did feel that something was missing and the pain. I felt just like my heart was cut and bleeding... Still I am very sensitive about it. It did affect me. I never felt better knowing I'd had this done...

participant 16

disbelief:

> *we talked about it saying... 'I can't believe our mums did this!'...*
> *I felt let down... then angry...*
>
> participant 30

and anger and hatred towards others:

> *I felt angry towards my mother and grandmother...*
>
> participant 9

> *I felt I hated the woman after, I also felt annoyed and angry*
> *towards my neighbours and cousins...*
>
> participant 5

> *I hated her after she had done it ...*
>
> participant 27

> *for the actual operation there was an old woman... I hated her*
> *then, I hate her now. I still don't say hello to her now she's still*
> *alive...*
>
> participant 9

Psychological effect of ceremony and celebration

The level of ceremony and celebration accompanying circumcision varied greatly amongst the women. For many, parties were given with lavish foods prepared, singing and dancing, and the girls were adorned with gifts and new clothes.

For some, the celebration, support, and pampering were enough to compensate for any hardship:

> *at first it was very hard and very painful... but I felt happy*
> *because I had presents and all...*
>
> participant 11

> *that was a nice time... the nice things made it ok. The bad things*
> *of the operation were that it was a bit painful... but it just takes*
> *half an hour. Before and after were nice times so I felt happy...*
>
> participant 7

> *after half an hour or less I started to feel the pain... I couldn't*
> *urinate, I couldn't walk... At the same time though, I forgot all*
> *this, because of my new clothes, henna, and visitors in the*
> *house...*
>
> participant 45

Had a few difficulties passing water but in those three days, I was busy counting my money, looking at my henna, and friends came too... I don't remember any part of the operation at all...

participant 8

we had party, gold, henna...these things kids love...

participant 39

they bought us nice gold and bangles. My grandma gave us nice bangles. Had henna put on...

participant 4

For others this pampering was not enough to distract them from their suffering:

had henna, jewellery, new clothes but couldn't enjoy this...

participant 54

the first day I refused everything. People gave me money, food, drink, because I was very scared...

participant 17

I cried for four or five weeks afterwards... I never ate anything I was so sick. I took it so hard, not like the other girls. For me it was so difficult. I didn't have an appetite after. Other girls were playing again before me but I became very nervous...

participant 55

Many received no special treatment but were just made to rest and perhaps fed specific foods that are supposed to assist with the healing:

I didn't have any presents. Just special foods were cooked, hot, hot foods supposed to make the healing better...

participant 44

we had to eat certain foods. There were no presents or parties. Afterwards, we had to stay in bed...

participant 30

Psychological sequelae at menstruation

During adolescence it is not uncommon for infibulated girls to suffer from the excruciating pain of restricted blood flow. Those who reported suffering from menstrual problems recalled how they would dread their time of the month, becoming anxious about the pain and discomfort:

severe pains with period...difficulty passing blood...tightness in stomach...nausea which would help blood come out...used to feel very down...

participant 1

Psychological sequelae in anticipation of and following marriage

The terror and anxiety in anticipation of their wedding night, has been acknowledged in a number of other studies (Kennedy, 1970, Boddy, 1982; El-Dareer, 1983b; Lightfoot-Klein, 1990) and was widely reported:

the anxiety and worry in the month before marriage was terrible.... you never escape that feeling of anxiety not knowing if you will have problems or not. That fear can change you...that fright for the month before I married changed my life. This fright was worse than the actual circumcision time, because I had so many fears... I felt nauseous all the time with anxiety...on my wedding night; I sprayed anaesthetic spray to numb my genital area, so that I did not feel anything. I was opened half on the second day. The actual pain from intercourse went on for about three months...

participant 38

For many, the first painful experience was enough to put them off sex:

there was no enjoyment for me and that put me off, and I would try to stay away...

participant 19

it was extremely, extremely painful, and I hated myself and my sexual organs. I was unable to enjoy it at all... Got a little better with time but I avoided sex whenever I could...

participant 16

and many felt that it was still problematic for them even now:

until now I do not feel pleasure and I do not like it, I never have an appetite for sex... even when I was younger... My husband used to beg me and chase me around...

participant 55

I always feel cheated out of more sexual pleasure....

participant 15

These feelings, however, may also be a consequence of being 'between cultures', as this may force circumcised women to view themselves in a completely different way. In the UK, circumcision often equates to 'suppression of sexuality', while in Sudan and Somalia (and other FGM-practising countries), it is often the essence of sexuality. This discrepancy can translate into circumcised women feeling alienated as they realise that physically, they cannot fit into the norms of the society at large. Some women felt that their difficulties around sexual intercourse affected their confidence and self esteem:

> *loss of confidence...*
>
> > participant 55

> *your self-esteem goes down as you feel you cannot do sex properly...*
>
> > participant 49

Psychological sequelae in anticipation of and following childbirth

In Somalia, de-infibulation is routinely carried out prior to delivery to facilitate the birth. In parts of Sudan, it is common practice for women to be re-infibulated following delivery. This cycle of circumcision, sexual intercourse, pregnancy, de-infibulation, re-infibulation, often continues with each successive birth and may, consequently, give rise to mental trauma.

For those women who experienced childbirth in the UK, many reported feeling very worried in the months before about whether health professionals would be familiar with the procedures for delivering their baby:

> *I thought a lot and worried a lot about how it would be with the baby...*
>
> > participant 35

> *I saw my sister when she had her baby and I would dread being in that situation...*
>
> > participant 9

Others felt their delivery was not handled well and they suffered:

> *the doctors came but had to call another because they didn't know* (how to deal with me)...
>
> > participant 26

> *my first baby I had, they knew nothing at all and it was very difficult...*
>
> > participant 55

Psychological sequelae in anticipation of future physical complications of circumcision

There is also the mental anguish reported by some women from a fear of what may happen in terms of problems they may face in the future:

> *how and when you will have problems is not predictable ... problems can appear at any stage in the lifecycle... those who don't have problems early on may suffer later. But you never escape that feeling of anxiety, not knowing if you will have problems or not. That fear can change you...that fright for the month before I married changed my life. This fright was worse than the actual circumcision time, because I had so many fears... I felt nauseous all the time with anxiety...*
>
> participant 38

> *it was a big worry, marriage and pregnancy time... then there are the problems with urine which doesn't always come out when you go to the toilet so you have leakages and have to keep going... half of my life has been affected by it...*
>
> participant 37

Psychological sequelae following ongoing recollections of the original circumcision operation

There are several reports from case studies of repressed memories previously inactive and unacknowledged being triggered by reminders such as television programmes or children screaming (McCaffery, 1995).

Almost three quarters of the women reported having experienced recurrent intrusive memories during a significant part of their lives and 49 per cent felt they were still plagued by such recollections today. Memories were often triggered by various objects:

> *knives...*
>
> participant 48

> *knives... even when cooking...*
>
> participant 44

> *the house is a reminder...*
>
> participant 1

> *when I see a razor... because mine was performed with a razor...*
>
> participant 22

They were also triggered by events:

one month before marriage I was very affected... the anticipation of what might happen...

participant 38

after my first child, I lost a lot of blood and used to have the same shivering feeling I had when I was actually circumcised...

participant 26

when discussing it... like today...

participant 10

when I see others done (being circumcised)...

participant 29

and situations:

when I used to travel back to the village in the winter I would associate the travelling with the anxiety I had back then...

participant 55

in my work as a midwife...

participant 38

Nearly three quarters of the women recalled how at times, when they had been plagued by recollections of the event, it had led to feelings of distress:

I couldn't stop thinking about it and cried a lot...

participant 35

when I saw knives I would feel sickly and sweaty... it was like a nightmare.. horrifying... worse than a horror film...

participant 44

Over two thirds reported still feeling distress when reminded of the event even today.

when discussing it... I feel stressful...fearful... and have a tightness in my chest...

participant 10

Many women recalled how they would try to avoid thinking about the event and would go as far as avoiding certain activities and situations:

razors and sharp objects...

participant 26

I would avoid sex...

participant 12

tried to escape from sex... I would find excuses... sleep early... go out... or study

participant 14

Some still avoided things:

certain TV programmes... I will not watch something on circumcision...

participant 38

I still remember the midwife... whenever I see her I just run... I never stay with her in one room...

participant 19

I feel different from others so I keep away from people...

participant 45

talking about it like now... I don't want to remember... I want to forget... please don't ask me anymore...

participant 48

Over half the women felt that the whole experience had affected their range of emotions for a long time afterwards and a quarter felt that this was still the case:

no more happiness... I became such a nervous person... it made me very wary about people...

participant 53

I couldn't even laugh in the month before marriage...

participant 38

Almost three quarters of them felt their experiences of circumcision and the mental pain that tormented them was often expressed through irritability or outbursts of anger, and almost half the women felt that this was still the case:

I feel not normal... other girls can become pregnant and have sex... but not me...why not me?

participant 40

you feel angry as to what's happened to you... Why?... What did I do to deserve this?

participant 44

very angry... I don't want to see that pain on anyone's face...

                                                        participant 18

Over half of the women reported feeling guilty about the effect that circumcision had on others to this day, and many felt they had no right to be complaining:

especially when I remember my sister's difficult experience...

                                                        participant 18

you always think your problem may not be much compared to what others may have...

                                                        participant 35

Whilst two thirds of the women had felt disillusioned and let down after they had been circumcised, over half still felt this way. Many blamed their parents or grandparents:

my grandma who did it against the will of my mother and father...

                                                        participant 12

society and my parents... but mainly my parents...

                                                        participant 16

why didn't my mother rescue me?...

                                                        participant 38

Some blamed the society or culture:

the culture... especially now since I know it's not religious...

                                                        participant 35

society not my parents... because it's a cultural thing...

                                                        participant 10

towards the culture... I hate myself for being Somali...

                                                        participant 55

Others blamed those that carried out the operation:

the women who do this...

                                                        participant 26

when I remember the man who did it... I feel I'd like to kill him... he was educated... a doctor... he should have known better...

                                                        participant 17

Others described the torment of not having anyone to blame:

you blame everything one by one... the religion... the culture... the relatives... Why did mother let it happen?... but it's all inside because you can't explain...

participant 45

I feel let down but there's no one to blame...

participant 20

you feel angry but don't know whose responsibility it is... they were ignorant and did it for our own good...

participant 14

because it's cultural it's part of life... there's no one to blame...

participant 38

Sadness and depression resulting from the experience was also a common feeling reported by many women:

because if I wasn't circumcised I'd not have had these problems...

participant 14

I have had to take antidepressants to cope with this...

participant 42

A lot of cases of depression and anxiety were found to be driven by what Toubia (1994) has termed 'genitally focused anxiety and depression' characterised by constant worry over the state of the genitals:

mainly disfigurement... I was conscious about it as a teenager very much... although everyone had it done, I still felt disfigured... I guess in the same way that someone who had a big nose or something would feel self-conscious...

participant 15

I felt I was an abnormal shape...

participant 16

the scar is something that I have become conscious about since I have been in the UK...

participant 21

my body image because they didn't stitch (re-infibulate) *after birth... not used to it...*

participant 54

Many women also feel very sad about the ongoing practice of circumcision:

when I hear now that Sudanese women take their daughters back (to be circumcised)...

participant 13

I feel sad because I feel sometimes that things won't change...

participant 26

when I hear that someone (in the community) *is getting married I feel worried for them*

participant 31

II Prevalence of psychological trauma

As the women's experiences show, circumcision is perceived by some as threatening, harmful, and physically traumatic, giving rise to fear, helplessness and other psychological symptoms. Whilst symptoms for some women become apparent immediately following the operation, many seem to experience surges in psychopathological symptoms at various stages throughout life. This pattern of distress and the symptoms experienced are synonymous with that of Post-Traumatic Stress Disorder (PTSD).

PTSD is the only anxiety disorder whose aetiology is associated with a known external event. The diagnostic criteria from DSM-IV identify the essential feature of PTSD as the development of characteristic symptoms following exposure to an extreme form of traumatic stress (American Psychiatric Association, 1994). This usually involves actual or threatened death, serious injury, threat to one's physical integrity, witnessing an event that involves death, injury or a threat to the physical integrity of another person, learning about unexpected or violent death, serious harm, or threat of death or injury to a family member or other close associate. The person's response to the event must involve intense fear, helplessness or horror (DSM-IV, 1994). Although PTSD symptoms usually begin soon after the event or within the first three months, there may be a delay of months, or even years, before psychological reaction becomes apparent.

Prevalence of PTSD

The Clinician Administered PTSD Scale (CAPS) was administered to all the women in my study to determine the prevalence of current PTSD (i.e. *ongoing* symptoms of PTSD at a clinical level), and lifetime PTSD (i.e. clinical levels of PTSD experienced at some point during their lifetime) specifically stemming from their experience of circumcision.

Of the women interviewed, less than one tenth were found to be suffering from current PTSD, whilst over a quarter had suffered lifetime PTSD. All participants showing current and lifetime clinical levels of distress had experienced the severe-type circumcision. To understand the severity of this, comparisons can be made with general population prevalence rates. Kestrel et al (1995) indicated lifetime prevalence of PTSD in a general population sample to be approximately 7.8 per cent; incidence of lifetime PTSD within this group of severely circumcised women is significantly high.

Not everyone experiencing similar negative life events goes on to develop PTSD. Certain risk factors predispose individuals to develop a stress reaction; likewise, despite similarities in their experiences of circumcision and significant physical complications in most severely circumcised women, physical complications alone do not predispose individuals to develop clinical levels of PTSD, as indicated by the following figure.

Severe Type FGM

Post-circumcision
physical
complications

?

PTSD   No PTSD

Figure 3: The role of post-circumcision physical complications in the development of clinical psychopathology

III Predictors of psychological trauma

The final phase of my study looked at factors differentiating those women who went on to develop *clinical* levels of PTSD from those who did not. Since coping and appraisal have both been cited in the PTSD literature as factors influencing the likelihood or not of developing a stress reaction to a stressful event, all those who had been subject to severe-type circumcision, were asked about coping strategies used and about overall appraisal of their circumcision experience.

Appraisal

Women's overall appraisal of their experience of circumcision was assessed, looking at their attitudes towards the practice, its importance, the overall impact on their life and on the lives of other women and whether they felt the practice should continue in any form. Comparisons were made between the responses of women diagnosed with lifetime PTSD (referred to as the trauma group), and those who did not meet a lifetime clinical diagnosis (the non-trauma group).

Importance of the practice

The majority of the women felt that circumcision in any form was not at all important:

> *...no need to do it... God made us like this. If there was no need for bits of our bodies, they wouldn't be made. I don't believe in all theories of circumcision. Before I grew up, I thought it was normal but it's not done in many Muslim countries...*
>
> participant 1

> *... it's putting girls through hell for no reason...*
>
> participant 44

> *...it has so many complications physical and mental so it's not only unimportant but a really brutal tradition that people stick to...*
>
> participant 16

> *...how can it be...?*
>
> participant 14

> *...it's part of the culture but in my opinion it is not important and should be stopped...*
>
> participant 26

> *... not good because when you get married and have children there are huge problems...*
>
> participant 48

Some felt there were some benefits to be gained – particularly from the point of view of hygiene:

> *...maybe for reasons of cleanliness...*
>
> participant 10

...from the point of view of cleanliness...

participant 39

One from the trauma group felt it did have some cultural significance:

...important from a cultural perspective...

participant 31

Overall impact on life

Women in the trauma group were significantly more likely to rate their experience of circumcision as having had a more negative impact on their lives, in comparison to the non-trauma group:

...because of the very bad experience I had after the operation... and then my sexual problems have been a big part of my life... 70 per cent of my life has been affected...

participant 14

...I thought it was normal, but when I started my period, got married, and had my baby and had all problems, I realised...

participant 20

...that fright for the month before I married changed my life. This fright was worse than the actual circumcision time, because I had so many fears... I felt nauseous all the time with anxiety...

participant 38

... psychologically when you think about the reason behind them doing it (circumcising you), *which is in a sense because you cannot be trusted* (to be chaste)*...*

participant 45

For many, the threat was in anticipation of future problems: ...because of the problems I think I will face in the future...

participant 41

...so far, although I anticipate that I may have problems in future, because I think all married women experience problems...

participant 10

Complications in other women

When asked about perceived complications in other circumcised women, almost one fifth felt that only some women have problems:

I don't think most women suffer... I think it depends on the type of circumcision you have and also on who did it... Whether some specialist doctor or whether done rurally by anyone...

participant 14

I think some women do have problems at time of marriage and periods...

participant 17

Others felt the majority suffer:

I think most who have pharaonic circumcision do have problems...

participant 42

only some people who have sunna circumcision have problems... but definitely those who have pharaonic type do, physically and psychologically...

participant 30

almost all have problems... the main ones are at the time of marriage and childbirth... but how and when you will have problems is not predictable. Problems can appear at any stage in the lifecycle... those who don't have problems early on may suffer later ...

participant 38

the majority of women do experience problems sexually, psychologically and lots of stress before marriage and on the first few days after marriage and childbirth...

participant 13

most women do but I think they try to ignore it and also, since they have nothing to compare it with, might think it's normal...

participant 40

and some were not sure:

don't know...people are very different...

participant 5

Continuation of the practice

When asked if the practice of circumcision should continue the majority of women, including all those in the trauma group, said it should stop completely:

no! it's a crime... It's not human...

participant 1

Some felt it should continue but only in mild sunna form:

I think sunna is ok (without stitch)*, but everything else should stop...*

participant 27

but just sunna - it's important because of the culture. Pharaonic is no good...

participant 28

whilst very few were not sure:

if you tell me it is good, I will say continue... If you tell me it's bad I'll say stop. Medical scientific evidence is important...

participant 43

Coping

All the women in the study were asked how they felt they had coped with their experience of circumcision and whether any particular coping strategies had been more helpful.

Overall coping

Of the mildly circumcised group of women, only one reported having experienced any problems at all. Some mildly circumcised women felt very strongly that this form of circumcision has such negative connotations:

I feel sad when people say it's bad because I don't feel it has had a bad effect on me...

participant 43

Of the women who were severely circumcised, just under three quarters felt they had had problems but had somehow managed to cope. Many felt it was a case of having had to accept it and just get on with life:

you had to cope because of the culture...

participant 38

you are meant to be happy, accept it and not complain...

participant 44

I think because I don't focus on it and for me it's over and done with, I get on with my life, so I don't have any problems...

participant 30

Some felt they had coped some times but not others:

not very well initially, but now not much of a problem...

participant 12

there have been times when I have coped and other times when I haven't coped well. I used to feel I had so many problems and that I was alone in this and I also felt I was an abnormal shape...

participant 16

maybe when I was younger I didn't think about it, but when grown up I started to think about it... what I lost, and how it is bad...

participant 17

A few felt they had not coped well at all.

badly because it's something I had no control over...

participant 20

Coping strategies

The women were asked about coping strategies that had been instrumental in helping them to cope with their experiences. Various internal and external strategies were found to have been helpful including prayer and faith, adherence to it as a religious/cultural practice, community support, and family support.

Prayer and faith

Prayer and faith were helpful to a number of women:

I used to manage by crying ... and also praying which helped...

participant 1

Religious/cultural acceptance

Over two thirds felt that their acceptance of it as a cultural and/or religious practice had helped them to cope:

because everyone had had it done, you feel as though you are part of a group...

participant 26

there (Sudan), *women laugh and tease uncircumcised women... so you feel normal with it...*

participant 14

Community support

Availability of community support was felt to have been important in helping the majority of women to cope with their experience:

chatting to friends...

participant 29

talking to other women...

participant 32

talking with friends...

participant 27

Family support

Family support proved beneficial to over one third of the women:

> *I think I coped well because I was very well prepared from an early age. I was ten when I had it done and had seen and heard about it from my older cousins...*
>
> participant 35

> *the fact that my husband was understanding and also a doctor was very helpful...*
>
> participant 12

> *I talk to my husband...*
>
> participant 5

On comparing strategies used by the trauma and the non-trauma group, it was clearly apparent that more women in the non-trauma group had felt supported by the community, and able to talk about and share their experiences; community support within the trauma group had not been such a positive and helpful experience:

> *you cannot always complain, they think you are making it up...*
>
> participant 20

> *talking and complaining is not accepted. You had to cope because of the culture...*
>
> participant 38

> *I think you suffer in silence because you are meant to be happy, accept it and not complain...*
>
> participant 44

or had been unavailable because the women had moved away from their communities:

> *I think when you're young and within your community, it's not as bad as if you were living here* (in the UK) *and out of the community...*
>
> participant 44

> *when in the community if you have problems you can accept them. but if you are outside of your community you don't have the support so you think more and have no emotional support..*
>
> participant 49

> *in my society I feel normal because I know that most there have had the experience...*
>
> participant 45

A predictive model of trauma development post-circumcision

In order to explain the findings from my study, I have developed a model illustrating the development of clinical levels of PTSD.

Mildly circumcised women, although not free of complications, do not tend to suffer the same degree of post-operational physical complications as severely circumcised women, and are unlikely to experience PTSD post-circumcision.

However, within the group of severely circumcised women, whilst the majority experienced post-circumcision physical complications at various lifecycle stages, this in itself was not a direct predictor in the development of PTSD. As their experiences show, most women *did* experience quite profound levels of psychological distress, but variables such as 'absence of anaesthetic', 'recollection of the experience of circumcision as negative', and 'absence of community support' were found to be statistically significant determinants in the development of PTSD. Consequently, these variables have been termed 'mediating factors' in the model.

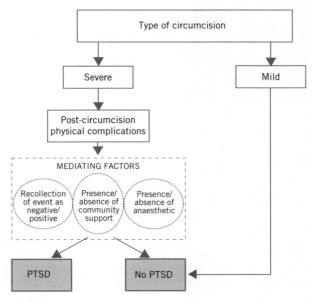

(Lockhat, H 1999)

Figure 4: A predictive model to explain the development of clinical psychopathology post-circumcision

Implications of the model

The study has given some idea about the prevalence and nature of psychological distress in women already circumcised arriving to the UK during adulthood, as refugees or immigrants. Whilst these cases form a significant proportion of circumcised women in the UK, there are also those born in the UK whose experiences will differ considerably.

Since the practice is illegal in the UK, the chances are that girls are likely to be either taken back to their parents' homeland and circumcised using traditional methods, or circumcised here – underground, and perhaps in the absence of any proper anaesthetic or surgical equipment. Whether circumcised illegally in this country or taken back to their parents' homelands, girls living as minority groups in this country are highly unlikely to have the same opportunities and access to community support. Limited counselling and support services currently available in the UK as a possible alternative may well exacerbate their feelings of isolation. Growing up in the UK, and exposed to the norms and attitudes of the society at large where the practice is not the norm and there is not a shared understanding of experiences by the majority, could mean further isolation. Cross-cultural disparity is, therefore, likely to be obvious and girls may consequently struggle to make sense of their experiences very early on in life. Bearing in mind the above model, psychological consequences and levels of PTSD could well be more acute and varied for those growing up as circumcised women in the UK.

CHAPTER NINE

WOMEN'S EXPERIENCES OF HEALTH AND SOCIAL CARE SERVICES

Introduction

This chapter explores women's experiences of health and social care in the UK. Although some women had positive experiences, the majority had negative experiences with health and social care services in this country (Lockhat, 1999). For many, the experiences not only tainted their views and attitudes towards health care professionals, but were also an important determinant in their development of PTSD. Some accounts are shocking but not surprising, given the little preparation currently provided for health care providers to meet the needs of circumcised women effectively.

Overall experiences

Positive experiences

A few women had received very positive information and support from health care professionals that they had found invaluable:

> *it wasn't easy… I didn't even know the name for circumcision in England…just had to explain to the GP, and he understood and wrote the name of it in English on paper… he also checked the type of circumcision I had, and explained…*
>
> participant 1

> *I told my doctor everything and she had read a lot about the issue but I was her first* (circumcised) *patient…*
>
> participant 47

> *my GP was understanding and I also had two very good midwives who comforted me… they have a good system at the Cath Locke Centre* (Manchester), *where the midwives helped a lot…*
>
> participant 54

Negative experiences

Of all those, including mildly circumcised women, who had experienced healthcare services in the UK, however, approximately three quarters rated their experience as having been very negative. This was either because of a lack of understanding or negative attitudes towards them by health care professionals, the inappropriate management of their care, or the stress of feeling isolated and/or alienated.

Lack of understanding by health care professionals

For many, the distress and anxiety was more to do with the lack of understanding by health care professionals and women's consequent lack of confidence in them:

> *when I had my baby, no one knew how to deal with it...*
>
> participant 20

> *with my second child* (born in the UK) *the doctors had no idea what to do and how to deal with it. The midwife would not stitch it back and I had to wait for four hours before the doctor came to stitch it...*
>
> participant 7

Inappropriate management of care

For others, it was more to do with inappropriate management of care on the part of the health care professionals, through lack of knowledge and experience:

> *some doctors would scare you by telling you that you were going to have lots of problems...*
>
> participant 35

> *the first child was very difficult because of the way they cut me... for twelve days I couldn't even sit. I couldn't feed the baby and things remained difficult after the birth... I felt very sick after and couldn't even look after my child...*
>
> participant 5

> *this was another nightmare. They cut me up and down and the sides ...*
>
> participant 44

Negative attitudes of health care professionals

This was the experience of several women in the study. One woman recalled going to see the nurse to have a routine smear test carried out:

> *I went for a smear test and because of my circumcision, I was told*

I needed to go to the hospital. The way the nurse looked at me, she was not understanding at all... and I felt very uncomfortable and embarrassed...

participant 16

One remembered her experience with her GP:

my GP said to me that it looks awful. I have also heard from other women that when they have been for examinations they are sometimes made an example of for other students to come and see and people don't always hide their expressions of shock...

participant 21

Another remembered how she felt when she had to be referred to the gynaecologist for problems with infection:

he (gynaecologist) was not very sympathetic, I didn't like the way he spoke to me about it. He was disgusted and didn't hide it...

participant 1

Several women vividly recalled the distress of being made to feel different when in hospital during childbirth:

with my first baby, they knew nothing at all and it was very difficult. I would hear them talking about me...

participant 55

I felt embarrassed when they were talking about my body...

participant 26

Feelings of isolation and alienation

Some women were aware that their circumcision made their experiences during childbirth different to non-circumcised women:

I was different from everyone else on the ward... but I couldn't tell them...

participant 19

Many felt very isolated and alienated:

when in the hospital, I felt very odd. All the other people (mothers who had given birth) were relaxed and happy. I felt there was something wrong with me...

participant 9

I felt different from other mothers because I had to stay in for ten days...

participant 20

I felt different as though I had done something wrong...

Participant 26

Perceptions based on hearsay

Many women, from hearing about other's negative experiences, described feeling fearful and anxious about how they would be seen and treated by health care professionals, and consequently avoided accessing health care services completely:

> *before I got married I used to avoid going for anything that would involve an internal examination because I was scared of explaining. Since marrying I have had to go...*
>
> participant 46

> *I'd avoid going to the clinic because I'd worry that the doctor would want to do an internal examination...*
>
> participant 35

> *I was sent a letter for a smear test but I ignored it...*
>
> participant 1

Improvement of services

When asked about improvements to health and social care services, more than three quarters of the women felt that significant improvements were needed. Suggestions for improvement included educating professionals, not only about issues around circumcision, but also about cultural sensitivity. Women felt they wanted to have confidence in the services available, more information and easier access to existing services, and more services and resources made available to support them. They also felt that community education and awareness raising about health complications arising from circumcision was important.

Educating and training health care professionals

Over two thirds of women felt that health care professionals needed to be more informed about the issue of circumcision and how to deal with it at a medical level.

> *here, (UK) I don't think they know how to deal with it. They need to know how to cut it for marriage time, and to have facilities for women to have this done...*
>
> participant 31

> *in Manchester they know about circumcision, but in other places they haven't got a clue. I think it should be made a compulsory part of training for doctors, midwives etc...*
>
> participant 8

awareness needs to be raised about how to handle these cases, especially the best way of cutting at childbirth...

participant 54

perhaps health days at schools and colleges... and raise awareness in general. Instead of putting TV programmes about the issue on at unsociable hours, put them on when people will see them...

participant 30

Cultural sensitivity

As mentioned earlier, a lot of the women's distress and anxiety was exacerbated by professionals' attitudes towards them, and consequently, a high proportion of women felt that this needed to be addressed:

in Sudan, antenatal care was good because we could discuss things openly with the midwife...

participant 19

in Somalia, no one is surprised because everyone knows about it... Here, they talk...

participant 26

I think professionals should have links with community workers to discuss the issues...

participant 10

they shouldn't feel sorry for you... we don't want people to feel sorry for us, we want them to understand the reasons why it was done...

participant 45

the women have already suffered a lot... they need to feel they can approach health professionals with this...

participant 38

I really think they (professionals) need to approach the issue without looking down on the practice and on the culture. This is the main barrier... and to understand it as well... This would break the ice and then they would be able to give counselling to women...

participant 47

family planning centres should have counsellors available... but the term for the service should be 'well-woman clinic' as a lot of women feel embarrassed (about going to a family planning centre)...

participant 14

More confidence in existing services

Many also felt that they wanted to have more confidence in the services they were receiving:

> *there should be more people available to talk to because the way it is now, they maybe have services available once a week... and you have to first see an assistant/secretary and give them details etc... I don't like this because it removes the confidentiality...*
>
> participant 14

particularly during child birth:

> *women should be given more pain relief because of the level of stitching that is required, so this should be routine...*
>
> participant 15

> *women should be reassured that they will be taken care of twenty-four hours...*
>
> participant 30

> *women should be allowed to stay longer in hospital after childbirth because they have many problems and need more help to enable them look after their baby...*
>
> participant 6

> *by women having a personal midwife... being able to see the same one every time...*
>
> participant 54

More information and easier access to available services

Some women also felt that more information and advice was needed about self care:

> *more advice should be given to ladies e.g. after discharge from hospital on how to deal with the stitches... some ladies try to follow Sudanese traditions, which aren't right and don't help healing...*
>
> participant 55

and services available for de-infibulation and restoration:

> *more information on reversal operation and restoration practices are needed for us so that we know what is available...*
>
> participant 40

More services and resources made available

Many women felt that essential services were lacking for both physical care:

> *de-infibulation is important for many women, since many are pressurised by their husbands to get it done... de-infibulation is important too during marriage, but here women can not always get it done at short notice and are told three months... This can cause huge problems especially if the woman in the meantime manages to get pregnant because then doctors refuse to do it until labour time so they have to suffer all this time...*
>
> participant 38

> *instead of just talking about the issues and questioning all the time, they have to do something...*
>
> participant 26

as well as emotional care:

> *the most important thing here is community support... and because it is often lacking here people living here should have access to counselling services...*
>
> participant 3

Community education and awareness raising

Many felt that work needed to be done within the communities practising FGM. This included information about what may happen during a consultation:

> *information about what they can expect from the doctors here...how they will be dealt with, etc...*
>
> participant 10

as well as awareness raising about the nature of their circumcision and the effect it was likely to have on childbirth, medical procedures, and on the general well-being of women:

> *at a community level...talking to societies who do it about advantages and disadvantages and get them to think about the future of their daughters...*
>
> participant 45

Some felt professionals from the same cultural background could be instrumental in providing information:

> *professionals within the community are useful since they know the issues at a cultural and professional level...*
>
> participant 44

> *they should help Somali and Sudanese midwives to be able to register here and practise because they are very useful...*
>
> participant 20

CHAPTER TEN

WORKING WITH CIRCUMCISED WOMEN
ADDRESSING CULTURAL PROFESSIONAL, AND ORGANISATIONAL ISSUES

Introduction

This chapter deals with the important topic of how to work with and care for circumcised women. Most health care professionals have no knowledge or understanding of the issues. Others do not see it as a problem in this country. Yet the stakes are high particularly when quick decisions have to be made by professionals in emergency situations. Whilst some guidelines or position papers have been issued by the government and other professional bodies, these are sparse and lack the 'hands on' guidance and information that professionals desperately need when confronted with the issue in practice. This chapter focuses on addressing cultural, professional and organisational issues. For each area, good practice guidelines around what to do and what not to do are provided.

I   Understanding the cultural context

Challenging stereotypes

It is important to be aware that not all African communities practise circumcision, and that even within the countries that practise it, not all females will have been circumcised. Where women have been circumcised, understanding and awareness about their own circumcision is very varied. Many women do not know any other state, believing circumcision to be the norm for all women worldwide. To discover that all women are not circumcised could come as quite a shock. For others who may have been born in this country and gone through the ritual at a young age, there may be vivid, vague or no memories of it at all.

Women who are aware that they have been circumcised may not be aware of the type of circumcision they have had, or realise that physical complications they may be experiencing, may be secondary to their circumcision. Professionals should not therefore assume that women are experts on their circumcision, and should feed back their diagnosis as they would when treating any other ailment – in a non-judgemental, culturally sensitive manner.

In addition, whilst circumcision may have left some women traumatised, not all women will have been affected in this way. For those who may be experiencing psychological distress, this could be due to other factors in their lives, and professionals should refrain from making stereotypical assumptions and linking such distress to circumcision in the absence of a full assessment.

Unlike the immigrants of the 1950s and 1960s who were predominantly from South Asian and African-Caribbean countries, immigrants from the countries that practise FGM are relatively recent arrivals to this country. As new arrivals, they may still be coming to terms with British cultural beliefs, attitudes and traditions, and may not be fully aware of the legal stance around FGM, or indeed, about how the law works here. Many may have come from war-torn countries, with unstable, corrupt political regimes, where laws can be bypassed through bribery or contacts. Some may be non-English speaking and also illiterate in their own language. Professionals should, therefore, refrain from assuming that individuals are aware and knowingly committing an offence.

Understanding traditional practices

Traditional healing practices are still important to many Middle Eastern and African communities. Many still consult faith healers and depend on homeopathic treatments for their ailments. Others may engage in behaviours to ward off the 'evil eye', which continues to have a dominant influence in many cultures.

Professionals need to understand the importance of such practices. Some remedies may interfere with prescribed medication and these will need to be flagged up. Other remedies, however, may be harmless and perhaps psychologically beneficial to individuals, and by respecting these, professionals will be showing positive regard for the culture, which can only serve to strengthen trust and confidence. *(See box overleaf)*

II Understanding women's behaviour

Expectations

Expectation of what will happen in consultation may be different.

Don't assume...

- that all African women have been circumcised
- that women will be aware of the type of circumcision that they have had
- that women will be aware of links between their circumcision and any subsequent health complications
- that women will be familiar with complex terms and medical jargon
- that all will be aware of legislation around FGM
- that all will be aware of opposing beliefs and attitudes around FGM

Do...

- ensure that you are fully informed about FGM
- ask about circumcision as a routine part of the history, maintaining a casual, matter of fact tone
- be aware of, and able to identify and explain about the different types of circumcision
- spend time explaining how/why there may be physical problems because of circumcision
- use simple language and sketches to facilitate understanding
- explain to women about all options available to them which may ease any difficulties
- approach each case impartially and non-judgementally, and refrain from making assumptions, just as when working with any other referral
- respect individual beliefs around traditional healing practices but do not shy away from asking about remedies used
- advise *against* any remedies that may be potentially harmful or likely to exacerbate conditions whilst recognising the value of and respecting those that are not harmful

Some may not understand the process of consultation and may not see the relevance of history taking or physical examinations – the relevance of which may not be fully communicated by professionals. Others may expect and be willing to receive treatment in the form of medication only. In many African countries, health professionals are seen as people of authority, education and enlightenment and are held in very high esteem. As such, advice, if given in the right way, is likely to have a lot of credence for these women.

The family context

In western societies, emphasis is on the individual's right to make decisions about his/her life (the individualistic approach). In many other cultures, it is regarded as normal practice for family members to have a say and to influence the lives of individual family members. The importance of the extended family structure amongst some cultural groups reflects the collectivist approach. These sociological constructs are extreme examples on a continuum and can lead to radical differences in communication. Professionals need to be aware that whilst some women will leave decisions about their health care to their husbands or families, others may appreciate time on their own to express their own opinions and views, and such opportunities should therefore be offered.

Cross cultural communication

General interaction

Whilst in western cultures medical consultations tend to be formal, brief and to the point, in Middle Eastern and African cultures, it is regarded as bad manners not to enquire after one's family or general health. Professionals should therefore bear this in mind when working with communities from these backgrounds, as this initial banter could be important in making individuals feel comfortable and engaged.

Self-expression

In the West, people are not only taught to express themselves from a very young age but are also encouraged to think of themselves as on an equal par with others – including with those older than themselves, or those in positions of authority. It is common, for example, for children to be asked their opinions, and openly express their disagreements, emotions and feelings. This kind of socialisation does not exist in all cultures or traditions where instead, the norm may be to be tolerant of one's disagreement or discomfort, particularly in the company of elders or authority figures. This translates into the way that individuals conduct themselves and communicate verbally as well as non-verbally. A good example of this is eye contact. In the West, eye contact is a mark of confidence, respect and attention, whilst in other cultures; it is often seen as a mark of utter disrespect.

Some women, therefore, may not be forthcoming with information or expression (verbal or non-verbal) in the way that health professionals may be used to; they may find it difficult to handle questions about their thoughts and feelings, and may not openly acknowledge or complain about pain and discomfort. Professionals should not, therefore, rely on familiar verbal and non-verbal cues to form their medical opinions but should familiarise themselves with other methods of gauging this, e.g. through use of diagrams or visual rating scales.

Modesty

Professionals should be mindful about women feeling uncomfortable at seeing male professionals to discuss intimate 'female' issues. Other women may not have any preference. Some may feel awkward answering questions of an intimate nature in the presence of their spouse or other family members, and this should be considered.

Don't...
- make stereotypical assumptions about family contexts
- assume all women will be bothered by the gender of the health professional
- rely on eurocentric non-verbal cues as indicators of how women feel

Do...
- be mindful of family dynamics
- provide opportunities for women wanting to speak to professionals in privacy
- bear in mind that individuals may not necessarily be in a position to make decisions about health matters there and then, as they may need to consult with family members. This may slow down the process, but the context must be understood and respected
- be aware of important cultural differences in communication
- use alternative methods of gauging thoughts and feelings, e.g. through use of diagrams, analogue scales, symbols, or other creative methods

III Addressing professional issues

Communication

Communication is based on a two-way process and, to be effective, professionals do not only have to understand and be aware of women's behaviour but, perhaps more importantly, need to be mindful about how they themselves are coming across to the women both verbally and non-verbally.

Dignity/Respect

Professionals are bound by medical ethics stipulating that all patients should be treated with dignity and respect. This includes the need to be sensitive and non-judgemental about other individuals' cultural beliefs irrespective of one's own culture, attitudes and beliefs. Whilst there are certain standards that are applicable to all individuals from every background, within some ethnic groups additional consideration may need to be given to communication, privacy, modesty and confidentiality in order to ensure dignity and respect. Once aware of cultural differences when working with minority or religious groups, it is not just a case of tolerating, respecting, or being professionally sensitive about people's different cultural practices and beliefs, but more about the need to understand that these represent a whole way of life for such groups.

Terminology

Professionals must keep in mind that women's attitudes towards circumcision are very varied. To some, being circumcised is a civilised act often associated with respect and status in their cultures and countries of origin. For professionals to refer to circumcision as barbaric, unnecessary, and mutilating, or to show their distaste non-verbally, can be regarded not only as derogatory and demeaning, but highly unprofessional. This may not only have repercussions on the therapeutic relationship but may also alienate women, deterring them from seeking help and support from health professionals. For those women perceiving the whole experience of circumcision as negative and damaging and who already feel sad, bitter and distressed, referring to their bodies as 'mutilated' could reinforce the humiliation and further any psychological damage. Professionals should use non-derogatory terms and, perhaps, find out the local terms used by women themselves.

Confidentiality

It is important for professionals to maintain professional standards including confidentiality at all times. Circumcised women are often concerned when medical students, nurses, or other professionals are called in to an examination to look and learn about circumcision. Many women have heard stories about women being photographed for research and training purposes. Such fears can contribute to levels of anxiety, making some women reluctant to be examined or, indeed, to seek help from their health care service. Privacy and discretion should be strictly adhered to and proper informed consent must be obtained before any professionals, over and above those that are essential, are called in.

Interpretation and translation

This is a common obstacle professional's face when working with minority ethnic communities in general. Whilst not ideal, it is common to find health care professionals using family members to act as interpreters during a consultation, either for reasons of convenience or due to a lack of interpreters. Whilst this may be unavoidable in some circumstances, some women may feel awkward and inhibited when having to discuss intimate problems through family members. Similarly, children and adolescents wanting to communicate their distress may not be at liberty to do so. Furthermore, unfamiliarity of medical terminology, misunderstandings of questions posed, or personal attitudes towards questions can lead to inaccurate transmission of information.

Emergency, unplanned, or unexpected consultations may prove more problematic in terms of accessing interpreters. Whilst not ideal, it should be possible to get around this through use of services such as Language Line, where services can be accessed twenty-four hours a day. For planned appointments, arrangements for face-to-face interpreters should be made. Efforts should be made to ask women if they are happy with the interpreter present, as there may be issues arising from the interpreter being from the same family or clan, or indeed from a rival group. Where possible, arrangements should be made for professionals to meet with interpreters in advance of a consultation. Where professionals have not used interpreters before, advice and assistance should be sought.

Whilst professionals may not be able to communicate verbally with individuals, they should acknowledge the importance of non-verbal communication which, in the absence of any direct dialogue, will convey strong messages to women about whether professionals are friendly, approachable, and trustworthy.

Lack of support and supervision

Dealing with FGM issues can be stressful for all the reasons outlined above. Whilst some professionals may have the skills to work competently and confidently, others may find it a difficult area either because they lack the skills and knowledge, or find it a difficult issue to reconcile with their own personal beliefs and attitudes. Support systems are not always adequate or available for professionals who are left instead to struggle with the issues themselves.This further alienates them and puts them off from wanting to get involved. Service providers should ensure that appropriate training and support are provided to health care professionals.

Don't...

- refer to the practice as 'genital mutilation' when discussing the issue with women
- make assumptions that because a woman cannot speak the language that this bypasses the need to gain her consent to use her for training purposes
- make assumptions that because women do not speak English, that they are uneducated or lack understanding
- rely on family members accompanying women to a consultation to interpret
- use children as interpreters
- use male interpreters for discussing intimate issues
- work without access to systems of supervision or support

Do...

- familiarise yourself and use terms that women use in their own language to refer to circumcision
- be aware of issues around medical ethics
- keep examinations to a minimum
- keep the number of professionals present during examinations to the bare minimum
- familiarise yourself with how to access interpreters in your service
- consult guidelines on how to use interpreters effectively in a consultation

continued overleaf...

...continued

- try to use the same interpreter for ongoing consultations with women and families to maintain consistency, continuity and confidentiality
- explain about the guidelines around confidentiality prior to the consultation in the presence of the interpreter and the service user
- use facilities such as Language Line where face- to-face interpreters are not easily available
- seek peer supervision from colleagues, bearing in mind issues around confidentiality
- access supervision/support from other organisations or neighbouring regions when it is not available or adequate locally

IV Acknowledging and addressing sensitive issues

FGM: a 'race' issue?

Some professionals see FGM as a 'race' issue and tiptoe around it or shy away from getting involved. Responsibility is often left to black colleagues in the team, who are seen as better qualified to deal with such issues, perhaps for no other reason than their colour or cultural background. Others find it difficult to reconcile the practice of FGM with their own personal beliefs and attitudes, or find the whole issue so personally painful that they are unable to address it. Professionals need to acknowledge and address these sensitive issues.

Prejudice and discrimination

Prejudice and discrimination is still rife amongst many people and within organisations. In its crudest form, it includes the refusal of help, or stereotypical and often derogatory comments being made directly to individuals (as seen in chapter nine). More subtle examples include negative comments or jokes being made about circumcised patients to other colleagues. Legal mechanisms exist in the form of the Race Relations Amendment Act (2000), which requires that all staff undergo appropriate training and are aware of discriminatory practices and behaviour. Professionals should ensure that they are provided with training.

Bearing in mind the high esteem bestowed upon them, health care professionals are in an influential position and have a unique opportunity to help women. It is important, therefore, that professionals do not waste this opportunity by allowing their own beliefs and attitudes to alienate women through their own behaviour. Encountering racism in a place that may have been perceived as a safe haven may be all the more devastating and exacerbate their sufferings.

The double standards issue

Many professionals, whilst aware of the controversial debates and issues around FGM, may not know how to deal with them. Of particular relevance is the issue of double standards. Whilst legal in some countries and in some states of America, requests by women in the UK for re-infibulation following childbirth are outlawed on the grounds that this is damaging to the health and wellbeing of women. For women to whom circumcision is the norm, this can be difficult to accept and damaging to their self-image, particularly since they may find countless examples of people choosing to do things to their bodies which could equally be regarded as brutal, barbaric, and damaging. Such practises include breast enlargement or reduction, face-lifts, operations to remove ribs to achieve a slimmer form, etc., which, in the UK, are perfectly legal for consenting adults. Whilst some health care professionals will undoubtedly find themselves having to deny requests for re-infibulation, it is vital that this is done sympathetically.

Don't...

- adopt a 'no problem here' approach
- see FGM as an issue for black colleagues and expect them to be experts in this area
- ignore the double standards debate around FGM
- take a hard-line approach and focus solely on legislation

Do...

- familiarise yourself with the cultural context of FGM
- acknowledge that some black colleagues may be able to offer a unique insight and ask for their advice and ideas
- read up and understand the law around the issue
- deal with FGM as you would any other complex issue

continued overleaf...

...continued

- familiarise yourself with your organisations legal responsibilities under the Race Relations Amendment Act (2000)
- be aware of and acknowledge your own feelings and opinions
- take action and challenge colleagues about racist remarks and attitudes
- handle the issues sensitively and non-judgementally
- acknowledge women's feelings of anger and frustration
- understand potential psychological effects of not being allowed to adhere to cultural practices
- discuss the legal implications with women
- respect the double standards debate, understanding and acknowledging frustrations
- seek supervision, support, and advice from colleagues
- seek advice and reassurance from your local community organisations
- be aware of the implications of professional mismanagement on physical and mental health

V Organisational issues

As seen in chapter nine, many women's experiences of healthcare services in the UK have, on the whole, been very negative. The general impression is that their needs are not understood or appreciated, and that they are looked down upon. A number of barriers continue to exist within services and much still needs to be done:

Barriers to care

Institutional racism

Whilst steps are being taken at national and local levels to deal with institutional discrimination in various shapes and forms, prejudice and discrimination within institutions is still rife, as highlighted by the Stephen Lawrence Inquiry Report (Macpherson, 1999). Circumcised women are likely to be faced with a triple jeopardy. Firstly, because of their colour, secondly for being female and thirdly, for being circumcised. Research on the experiences of ethnic minorities within the health care service has shown that institutional racism exists in all aspects of the service, from employment to service delivery (DoH, 2003).

Lack of interpreters

This is a fairly common obstacle faced by organisations all over the country, and is not necessarily due to a lack of available interpreters, but more often to do with funding. In areas where ethnic minority communities form only a very small percentage of the population, interpreters sometimes have to be brought in from other towns/cities, which often takes time to organise. It is not always possible to find interpreters for all languages. Where interpreters are available, they may be male, or from the same community or ethnic background which can inhibit women from speaking openly. Furthermore, many interpreters will not have medical/counselling backgrounds, and may themselves struggle with vocabulary. However, interpreters must be provided where necessary, as depriving women of the opportunity for a proper consultation is unfair, unethical and not in line with guidelines.

The new Race Relations Amendment Act (2000) makes it a legal duty for statutory health care providers to develop and implement Race Equality Schemes outlining how they will meet the needs of black and ethnic minority communities, as well as promote race equality in employment. Institutions are likely to fail in their legal duty by not having proper interpreting and translating facilities and training for staff to enable and empower them to provide services effectively.

Lack of understanding

Services need to consider the practical issues arising from cultural practices. Whilst a number of African well-woman clinics have been established in some parts of the country, offering a drop-in service for women to have reversal operations carried out, they are not geographically accessible to all women. Although some hospitals now also offer reversal operations, this is deemed a low priority operation, and women sometimes have to wait six months for this to be carried out. Marriages amongst these communities are often arranged very quickly and take place within a short space of time. Furthermore, consummation on the wedding night is deemed essential from a cultural and traditional perspective. Services need to appreciate and be sensitive to the fact that women may not always have six months to be able to wait, but may be married within a month. Marriages are unlikely to be cancelled, even if the facilities are unavailable, and the chances are that alternative ways of opening the circumcision scar will be used.

Don't...

- ignore the legally enforceable requirements of the Race Relations Amendment Act (2000) for service delivery and employment
- delay the provision of training as required in your Race Equality Scheme particularly to frontline staff and key personnel

Do...

- ensure interpreters are easily available in areas where there is a high demand
- set up interpreter banks jointly with other agencies or with neighbouring regions in areas where demand is low or resources are scarce
- have systems in place to identify language barriers as early as possible (i.e. at the appointment-making stage) so that arrangements can be made well in advance to mobilise interpreters
- implement anti-discriminatory policies and procedures and demonstrate your commitment to valuing diversity publicly
- be mindful about the barriers to accessing services that many minority ethnic groups often face and look at ways of addressing these
- consider the cultural context and individual circumstances when prioritising procedures such as reversal operations

Turning failure into success

Diversity communication

In order to engage with women and encourage them to seek help, services need to ensure that they are sending out the right messages. This can be achieved by services understanding the needs of the different population groups living in the locality that they serve, and incorporating diversity into local service provisions. Efforts to acknowledge and celebrate diversity send out strong messages to communities and make organisations relevant to them. This helps in building community partnerships, and winning confidence and trust. Whilst some organisations have started to diversify by incorporating multi-cultural themes in posters, pictures, and information leaflets, many have not yet recognised the value of integrating diversity in this way. This is particularly pertinent in areas where there are high concentrations of minority ethnic groups. These steps would help not only to break down barriers and demystify fears and anxieties that women may harbour about health care services, but would also mainstream and standardise practices and procedures.

An integrated service

Once a health or social care body is aware of the diverse populations it is serving, it should endeavour to prepare its facilities and institutions making them more responsive, sensitive, and effective for those groups. All communities deserve a best-value, high quality service that meets their needs. An organisation therefore fails in its duty if it has not prepared or planned to meet the needs of its diverse customers. In addition to having an internal strategy and delivery plan, organisations should also endeavour to work with other local partners through their local strategic partnerships (LSPs) to devise a local strategic multi-agency response to FGM.

Initiatives around training for relevant professionals, educational programmes and service needs must be considered in the overall strategic plan. This could also include creative initiatives such as issuing certificates, where requested, to young unmarried girls, verifying that the de-infibulation has been done on medical and health grounds. This could help to secure future marriage and family honour.

However the context must be clear and understood before devising, planning and executing any service. There is no doubt that a lot is known about the main minority ethnic groups in the UK, but a lot less is known about the FGM-practising communities. The dilemma facing many, as I have argued elsewhere (Lockhat, 1999b), is that of isolation (exacerbated possibly by the government's dispersal scheme), a lack of people to talk to about their problems, as well as experiences of racism and discrimination. These are real issues that need to be considered by health and social care agencies in the context of both service provision and community cohesion. It is, therefore, crucial that service planners and providers engage and involve these already marginalised communities at every stage of any process.

Linking with community and religious organisations

Services can build bridges with communities by forging links with the local community and religious organisations, as well as community support groups in their locality. Through such links, women can be informed about the services and facilities available to them, how to access these and where to go if services are not available in their local area. These links can also be used to mobilise religious leaders to help educate FGM-practising communities on the religious position. As the Manchester based community activist, Mohamed says:

> *the Somali community won't listen to people from different faiths but they would listen to the leaders at the mosque*
>
> Mohamed, 2003

Arrangements can also be made for professionals to go to places of worship and for community organisations to run workshops on general health issues for women.

Using communities as a resource

Health care services can employ local women from their communities to serve as advisors to health care professionals, not only with regard to FGM, but also on more general cultural issues. Many are trained nurses and midwives in their own countries, and can be given further training in counselling which, together with their knowledge, understanding and expertise, can be an invaluable resource. In addition to this, word of mouth is a powerful tool in transmitting messages within close-knit communities providing a real opportunity to make a difference by propagating the negative consequences of FGM. Health and social care services should not, therefore, underestimate the power of this invisible network and should take every opportunity to use it.

Don't...

- underestimate the power of community engagement
- underestimate the role of community and religious organisations in facilitating links with communities
- ignore the valuable resources available within the communities themselves

Do...

- look at the diverse population groups that your organisation is serving
- prepare facilities and organisations to ensure they are meeting the needs of all communities
- give consideration to communication strategies, i.e. posters, leaflets, notices, information booklets etc. available in different languages
- bear in mind that many may be illiterate, so ensure that there are visible displays e.g. pictures or artwork from their homeland that will be familiar to them and make them feel welcome
- form links with local community and religious organisations
- publicise the services that are available to assist with FGM through local community and religious groups
- arrange for professionals to deliver health workshops at local community and religious centres
- consult individuals within the communities and those who may be trained health or social care professionals who will be able to offer a unique perspective and invite them to participate in public/patient forums to give advice on policy, procedural issues around FGM, as well as insights into cultural issues
- liaise with your local strategic partnerships (LSPs) to devise a multi-agency/area-wide response to FGM

CHAPTER ELEVEN

WORKING WITH CIRCUMCISED WOMEN
ADDRESSING PHYSICAL AND PSYCHOLOGICAL NEEDS

Introduction

Whilst the previous chapter focused on addressing cultural, professional and organisational issues, this chapter looks at the specific physical and psychological needs that may arise at various lifecycle stages including childhood, adolescence, pregnancy, and older adulthood. Advice is given on how professionals should deal with these issues. The final part of the chapter looks at considerations that need to be made when engaging and working with families around difficult issues that may arise around child protection.

The advice given on medical problems within each section is more to do with managing interactions. Physicians will need to consult other sources of information for more in depth advice on medical procedures.

I   Children and adolescents

Professionals likely to come into contact with child and adolescent issues around FGM, are likely to include GPs, health visitors, paediatricians, genito-urinary medicine (GUM) health professionals, school nurses, teachers, Education Welfare Officers (EWOs), educational psychologists, child psychology and psychiatry services, social workers, Child and Adolescent Mental Health Services (CAMHS), family planning nurses, gynaecologists and various other health and social care professionals. Since the threat of FGM is also a recognised ground for asylum application, immigration officials, barristers and solicitors working within this field also need to have an adequate and appropriate understanding of the issues in order to make informed judgements and effective representation of their clients.

The discovery of circumcision on young children can be a very emotive experience for some professionals – particularly if they are not familiar with the procedure and the context within which it occurs. It is crucial therefore, to have a prior awareness and understanding around FGM, as well as an awareness of the importance of impartiality in one's reaction, irrespective of personal feelings and attitudes.

Physical problems that may be apparent during childhood and adolescence

Unless suffering from post-circumcision complications, circumcision will not generally come to light during routine medical examinations by GPs. It is only if a child is suffering from some serious ailment where a full examination *may* be carried out, that it *may* come to attention. Even then, mild (Type I) circumcision, which has minimal mutilation, will not be obvious.

Physical problems secondary to severe type circumcision during childhood and adolescence might include:

- wounds
- infections
- pain
- cysts
- urinary tract infections
- micturition (problems urinating)
- painful periods
- pelvic infections
- resistance to physical examination

How should physicians deal with the physical sequelae to FGM in young children and adolescents?

1 Physicians should treat medical problems, such as infection, as they would in any other situation. Whilst this may initially involve prescribing antibiotic medication without the need to carry out a physical examination, where examinations are carried out, they need to be mindful that the circumcised area may be very sensitive. Many girls will be extremely frightened, anxious and wary about having this area examined (driven by past experiences), and may be resistant to such examination. For others, it may trigger distressing memories or flashbacks of being circumcised. It is important, therefore, for physicians calmly to explain what they are going to do in advance, and minimise any physical examination.

2 If a child's presenting problem is secondary to circumcision, this should not be left unexplained; many parents may not make the link

between circumcision and consequent physical health problems. Time should be spent, therefore, explaining why it is that the child has the problem, using simplified language and diagrams to explain if necessary.

3 Even if the presenting problem is not secondary to circumcision, the circumcision should be acknowledged and the opportunity taken to educate parents in a very gentle, non-judgemental way, about the negative health consequences of FGM and the legal stance. Rather than outlining the practice as a violation of human rights, information should be focused on the negative health repercussions, which are likely to be more meaningful and pertinent to families.

4 Verbal advice should be supplemented with a very basic information sheet (available in their own language) if appropriate, outlining the health effects of FGM, as well as the legal position. Information should also be given advising where further advice and support can be obtained if required.

5 Arrangements should be made for girls and/or their parents to speak with specially trained individuals with an awareness of the issues, so that information can be clarified and any areas of concern can be discussed further. This is particularly important since women may feel awkward in speaking about the issue. Many may be illiterate and not able to benefit from information sheets.

6 Children and adolescents have the right to be treated with dignity and respect and in a confidential manner by health and social care staff. Information from consultations should not therefore be divulged to other agencies unless it is in the best interest of the child, or there are issues around child protection. Reassurance about confidentiality should be conveyed wherever possible, particularly with adolescents for whom such concerns may be more pertinent.

Additional physical health considerations when working with older adolescents

A number of additional physical health concerns may arise with older adolescents, who may present to GPs, well-women, or genito-urinary medicine (GUM) clinics, with questions or anxieties about sexual health issues, worries about HIV, or concerns about their circumcision. Many women feel comfortable attending GUM clinics, because of the self-referral, walk in system that operates, without the need to make an appointment. Furthermore, they do not have to disclose personal details, and are assured of heightened confidentiality.

1   When seeing adolescents for medical issues, clinicians should be careful in how they feed back their diagnosis, and should not assume that girls know they have been circumcised. Clinicians may need to spend some time explaining to the individual about the alteration to her anatomy whilst refraining from use of the terms 'normal', 'abnormal' or 'mutilation'.

2   If the problem she is presenting with is as a direct consequence of circumcision it will be important to explain what the problem is and why it has resulted, using drawings where possible to facilitate understanding.

3   Health advisors working in GUM and well-women clinics, are often specifically trained to offer specialised counselling around sexual health issues. If trained in FGM issues, they would be an invaluable source of support to circumcised women.

4   Guidelines on what to do if a girl under the age of consent is requesting a reversal operation can be found in the section on 'professional dilemmas' later on in this chapter.

Psychological problems that may be apparent during childhood and adolescence

Recently circumcised children born in the UK who may be struggling to make sense of their experiences, might well present with a number of emotional and psychological symptoms. From the model proposed outlining the factors important in determining the development of PTSD (as discussed in chapter eight), and from existing research documenting common reactions that children may display when traumatised (Pynoos and Nader, 1993; DeWolfe, 2001), it is possible to speculate, to some degree, about possible psychological repercussions.

Psychological repercussions secondary to physical difficulties may include:

-   difficulties urinating, necessitating frequent and lengthy trips to the toilet. This could mean late arrival to lessons and consequently impact on learning. This could also incur chastisement by teachers, and have negative consequences on self esteem

-   difficulty around menstruation leading to frequent absences from school. This could impact on opportunities for learning and achievement, and affect confidence and self-esteem

- difficulty maintaining personal hygiene at school. This could increase the likelihood of teasing and bullying. Religious and cultural importance of hygiene could increase anxiety and precipitate distress

Other symptoms of distress in very young children (one to six years) might include:

- heightened arousal (fear, anxiety, anger, sadness, agitation and confusion)
- startle response to sounds, pictures or situations
- freezing or sudden immobility of movement
- difficulty identifying feelings
- anxiety in new or unfamiliar situations
- general or specific fears or phobias
- separation anxiety and clinginess
- regressive behaviours (e.g. bedwetting, soiling, loss of acquired speech)
- depressive illness
- psychosomatic symptoms (e.g. headaches, stomach aches)
- nightmares or sleep difficulties
- sudden weight loss

In school-aged children (6-11 years), additional symptoms may manifest including:

- feelings of guilt
- preoccupation with danger
- repetitious traumatic play
- aggressive outbursts
- school avoidance
- marked changes in behaviour, mood and personality
- withdrawn, aloof behaviour
- general fear response
- loss of interest in activities
- marked loss of concentration

In addition, psychological distress following FGM may be exacerbated by other factors common to refugees, asylum seekers and immigrants, such as:

- linguistic, cultural, and religious differences between home, society at large, and school

- feeling trapped between two cultures; the pressures from their own community to keep to traditions, and those of the wider society to fit in and be like others
- racial, cultural, and religious discrimination.
- struggling to learn English which is their second language
- coping with responsibility e.g. being the primary interpreter for other family members.

Such symptoms could have knock on effects on peer relationships, confidence and self-esteem, as well as performance at school.

How should professionals deal with signs of psychological and emotional distress in young children and adolescents?

Girls who are struggling to make sense of their experiences, and who may see the world as threatening and unpredictable will need to receive clear messages from adults and others reassuring them that:

- they are in a safe place
- they are likeable, capable, and needed
- they can contribute to the school and community
- they are not alone, others are there to listen and help

At a proactive level, teachers can implement a number of strategies in the classroom that can be beneficial in helping children to cope with feelings of insecurity and anxiety, whilst also getting some of these messages across to them. These might include:

- providing a safe and nurturing environment
- providing clear expectations, consistency, and structure in their daily routines
- preparing them for change and facilitating transitions
- providing opportunities to do important tasks at school to increase confidence and raise self-esteem
- raising cultural awareness within the school/classroom, celebrating diversity and highlighting positive aspects of cultures to encourage a sense of pride and belonging
- recognising strengths and rewarding achievements
- acknowledging the potential impact of their trauma as a possible driving factor in any learning and/or behavioural problems

1 In areas where there are high concentrations of minority ethnic groups that practise FGM, schools should have a named member of

staff who is trained in the area of FGM, and knows how to deal with it professionally and sensitively. This lead staff member can then educate other staff members about the potential effects that it may have on the physical and emotional wellbeing of girls, and any tell tale signs they may need to be aware of. In high population areas, it may also be beneficial for school nurses to receive training.

2   Schools could also adopt a number of practical strategies, to help minimise distress and anxiety e.g. by providing facilities to assist with personal hygiene. Washing of the private parts after visiting the toilet is common practice amongst a number of communities. Schools can endeavour to make washing facilities available in the toilets, e.g. by providing plastic jugs in addition to toilet paper for this purpose.

3   If concerned about a child's emotional state, teachers should follow this up in the same way as they would for any other child needing specialist help i.e. through school nurses, school doctors, education welfare officers (EWOs), educational psychologists, and if appropriate, social services. As with all referrals to CAMHS teams (or to equivalent services), parental consent will be essential, and schools should enlist the help of interpreters and link workers where necessary.

4   Once referred for specialist help, professionals need to be mindful of cultural differences in the presentation of psychological distress. Where possible, input from professionals of the same cultural background, or with expertise in the cultural issues, can prove invaluable.

5   Many professionals describe FGM as a 'dilemma in child protection'. Aside from circumcising their daughters, there is likely to be no fault in any other aspect of their parenting. Whilst FGM is illegal in this country and professionals have a duty to take action, it is crucial not to jump to conclusions and trigger off child protection procedures in the absence of clear evidence. As we are all well aware, whilst done for the protection of the child, child protection procedures can be a very frightening and distressing experience for the whole family. Bearing in mind the cultural context within which female circumcision operates, it is likely to be even more distressing for these families. Guidelines about how to progress if professionals suspect a child has been circumcised should be available in the organisations ACPC guidelines. Further help and advice can also be obtained from FORWARD.

Additional psychological problems that may be apparent during adolescence

Girls with no recollection of having been circumcised, who later find out when examining themselves, may become preoccupied with memories and flashbacks, or may experience feelings of confusion, disbelief, anger, and blame, and have nowhere to turn to.

Since most media coverage on FGM is usually eurocentric and therefore extremely negative and derogatory, the effect on circumcised girls growing up here can be very detrimental. They may struggle to reconcile the attitudes and beliefs around the two cultures that they find themselves between. Those who may have been socialised to feel proud about being circumcised may now find themselves confused and unsure and begin to question the practice, the culture, their beliefs and identity.

Faced with constant media images of femininity and sexuality within western society, many may feel alienated, abnormal, and disfigured, and struggle with issues around body image. There may also be additional stresses facing this age group, including the distress and anxiety of being caught between two conflicting sets of cultures – where the culture of origin values virginity, modesty, and chastity, whilst the indigenous culture promotes pre-marital relationships, sexual freedom and expression. Some, who may have experienced significant physical problems secondary to circumcision, may be aware that reversal operations could help them, but may not be able to discuss this with parents and may not have the freedom or mobility to access these independently. This could precipitate depression, social withdrawal, feelings of shame, guilt and humiliation, sleep and eating disturbances, thoughts of revenge, rebellious behaviour at home or school and adverse repercussions on school performance.

Additional anxieties will tend to surface as women prepare to marry or engage in intimate relationships. Many may not be aware of services available for de-infibulation and may have concerns about whether they will be able to have sexual intercourse and whether they can use certain forms of contraception. Fear of humiliation may inhibit them from confiding their worries and anxieties to uncircumcised peers. They may feel isolated and not know where to turn to for advice.

Concerns may be focused around issues, such as:

- identity
- belonging
- conformity with peers

- body image
- sexuality
- attractiveness
- intimate relationships

Since most of these are typical 'normal' adolescent concerns, it may be difficult for professionals to identify when the issues are secondary to the experience of circumcision, as opposed to age-appropriate anxieties, which are a passing phase.

For those already married or in intimate relationships, there may be concerns and difficulties around sexual intercourse including:

- painful intercourse
- intrusive memories of their circumcision experience
- sexual dysfunction
- anger and frustration at not experiencing pleasurable sex the way they see it portrayed by the media, or in the way that they hear other women describe
- psychosomatic symptoms
- feelings of inadequacy
- low self-confidence and self esteem
- depression

How should professionals deal with these additional concerns?

1 Opportunities should be made for discussion of any issues or anxieties relating to circumcision, through careful prompting. Many adolescent concerns and anxieties may be secondary to physical concerns (i.e. about contraception use, services available for de-infibulation etc.) for which referrals to the family planning nurse will suffice, as long as these professionals have a basic awareness and understanding of the issues around FGM.

2 If it is felt that more specialised help is required from CAMHS, this should be discussed with the individual, bearing in mind that whilst some may find it useful to talk about their experiences, others may not.

3 It will be important to bear in mind that within some communities, emotional and psychological distress is not very well understood and acknowledged and there are taboos associated with accepting help. This is often due to a misunderstanding of what is involved when referred to such services, and professionals should, therefore,

be prepared to explain what they can offer and how it is that they might be able to help.

4 Information should also be given to women about what happens when a referral is made, in terms of who a referral might be made to, where they will have to go for appointments, how long it will take to receive an appointment, whilst also mentioning about guidelines around confidentiality.

5 For those women who are unlikely to accept or benefit from CAMHS referrals but where psychological distress is nevertheless clearly apparent, consideration should be given to alternative means of support. These might include providing information to individuals about community groups, women's groups, or other organisations.

6 Women should be made aware of reversal operations and reparation interventions, though professionals should ensure that women are under no illusion about regaining any sexual sensitivity. If wishing to go ahead with such operations, psychosexual counselling should be a standard part of the procedure pre and post-operation so that women's motives and expectations can be monitored. This should be done by a trained counsellor and, where appropriate, both partners will need to be involved.

7 For those experiencing significant sexual dysfunctional problems, advice should be given about services available to assist with such issues and, where appropriate, referrals should be made to specific agencies.

8 Where appropriate, translated information leaflets should be available for women to take away and read, covering the above issues. Opportunities should also be made available for women wanting to discuss any further issues face to face with professionals, competently trained to give advice in this area.

II Pregnant women

Physical and psychological problems that may be apparent during pregnancy

Health professionals likely to encounter FGM when working with pregnant women include GPs, midwives, and obstetricians.

Professionals need to be thinking about the needs of severely circumcised women antenatally, at the time of delivery, as well as post-partum. Unfortunately, it does not always come to light that a woman has been circumcised until the actual time of delivery. A woman herself may not necessarily volunteer this information for a number of reasons. These include fears about how she will be perceived and treated by health professionals, anxieties about the legal implications of volunteering such information, or not feeling comfortable about bringing up the issue themselves.

As some researchers have shown, prolonged and difficult labour can precipitate the development of PTSD (Ballard 1995). For circumcised women living as minority groups in societies such as the UK, there is more chance of experiencing prolonged and difficult labour, particularly when physicians lack experience or understanding. In light of this, consideration should be given to the provision of joint medical/psychological clinics antenatally, where psychological issues can be identified and dealt with early on.

How should professionals care for women antenatally?

1 Irrespective of how and when professionals become aware that a woman has been circumcised, it is crucial that they acknowledge their awareness to the individual in a calm reassuring manner. Even if they themselves are unsure of the procedures involved to facilitate the birth, they have a duty to instil confidence that she will be looked after throughout the pregnancy.

2 The role of midwives, and in some cases GPs, is crucial since it is they who tend to be the first port of call in taking a medical history. Since internal examinations are rarely carried out on women in the initial stages of pregnancy unless there are problems, it is important that GPs and midwives are familiar with the communities that practice FGM. Appropriate questions need to be asked as a routine part of the history taking, to determine as early as possible whether circumcision may be an issue (particularly when bearing in mind that de-infibulatory procedures are best carried out well in advance of labour – ideally at 20 weeks gestation to ensure complete healing prior to delivery).

3 On finding out that a woman has been circumcised, the GP and/or midwife should inform the obstetrician so that appropriate examinations can be undertaken and preparation made with regards to the birth plan.

4 Information conveyed to women at this stage should include careful explanation of the difficulties in providing obstetric care where there is inadequate access to the vagina. The option of

having a de-infibulatory procedure antenatally or at delivery should also be discussed, with the advantages and disadvantages pointed out accordingly. Clinicians should use diagrams when explaining how and why de-infibulation is necessary. They should also point out that the procedure is done using anaesthetic, as many women will have grave concerns and be reluctant to go ahead with the procedure, putting it off until delivery, out of fear of pain from the surgery.

5   Informed consent is necessary at all times and women should not be pressured into giving consent to de-infibulation there and then, as many will need to seek permission from their husbands or families.

6   For women seen antenatally, where the pregnancy is too advanced to perform de-infibulation, plenty of reassurance will need to be given about procedures at delivery. Clinicians should spend time discussing how de-infibulation at the time of delivery will be carried out. Whilst pelvic examinations in the interim may prove more difficult to do and are likely to be uncomfortable and extremely painful, women should be encouraged to relax and can be taught simple relaxation techniques to reduce anxiety and discomfort.

7   Provisions should also be made antenatally for women to talk through any anxieties about pregnancy and childbirth, and techniques such as relaxation can be introduced, which may go some way towards easing any resulting discomfort and pain.

How should professionals care for women at delivery?

1   For those unexpected cases where circumcision comes to light at the time of delivery, it is essential that all clinicians handle the situation correctly.

2   In areas where there is a high concentration of people from circumcision practising communities, hospitals should have named individuals who are aware of the issues at a cultural, medical and psychological level who can be contacted for assistance and advice.

3   Making the correct incisions is of crucial importance. A lack of knowledge about the correct procedure may lead to immense pain and suffering for days afterwards.

4   Professionals should bear in mind that the whole process of childbirth – which can be a traumatic experience anyway, can trigger off memories of the original experience of being

circumcised. As seen in chapter eight, a number of women reported feeling uneasy around knives and other sharp instruments, and care should therefore be taken with unfamiliar surgical instruments. Incidence of distress could be minimised if procedures are explained to the women in advance, prior to delivery, and if, in addition, arrangements can be made prior to delivery for them to see the delivery suite. In cases where professionals are not forewarned that a woman has been circumcised, they should be sensitive to these anxieties.

5 FGM is *not* an indication for routine caesarean sections to be carried out, due to maternal morbidity associated with this procedure.

6 Re-infibulation is outlawed in the UK. Suturing to repair tears should be carried out promptly after delivery in accordance with the RCOG guidelines.

7 Women unaware of the legal stance around re-infibulation, who have not had a discussion with professionals earlier on, may be puzzled as to why they have been left 'open' (unstitched). As mentioned above, it is crucial that this issue is raised in the early stages of pregnancy, so that women who follow the tradition of re-infibulation have time to get accustomed to the idea and can seek counselling where necessary. In the event that this issue has not been dealt with in advance, enough time must be allowed after delivery for this discussion.

How should professionals care for women post-partum?

1 Women post-partum will need information on how to deal with their de-infibulation wounds and/or any perineal trauma. Hygiene of the area to prevent against infection will be an important determining factor in the healing process. It is crucial that professionals do not assume women will be aware of how to deal with their wounds. Clear guidelines of care should be given with an indication of how long it will take to heal. Follow-up appointments should also be arranged to check whether wounds are healing.

2 Consideration should also be given to pain relief to minimise discomfort, which may be prolonged postnatally.

3 Information and advice may also need to be given to de-infibulated women on issues around menstruation, urination, and sexual intercourse, as experiences following de-infibulation for women for whom this is not the norm, will more than likely be very different.

III   Older women

GPs will be the health professionals most likely to encounter cases of circumcision in older women.

Physical and psychological problems facing older women

As mentioned previously, physical problems following infibulation are often ongoing and recurring. Problems that older women are likely to experience will be similar to that at other lifecycle stages. Calculus formation may become more acute with age, and menopausal problems including atrophy of vulval, perineal and vaginal tissues may also contribute to difficulties. Older women may be more reluctant to seek help from 'foreign' professionals, and more time may need to be spent engaging them.

Older women's views and attitudes towards circumcision are likely to be extremely varied, depending on their experiences. Many may well feel very passionate that it should continue. Some women may experience symptoms of psychological distress, as already described in the previous section. Others, whilst open to discussion, may passively acknowledge its ill effects, but see it as a cultural practice over which they have no control. For the majority of women who will have spent a significant part of their lives in their country of origin, however, FGM will be seen as the norm and a way of life that does not warrant any discussion. They are likely to be defensive and resistant to criticisms about the practice and harbour attitudes condemning double standards and 'western' supremacist views. Those speaking out against it are likely to be branded as 'westernised' in their outlook and may be ostracised from their communities.

Emotional and psychological problems may be present irrespective of the stance taken, i.e. whether in favour of *or* against the practice. Whilst this may come as a surprise to some people, professionals need to acknowledge that some women prevented from carrying out FGM on their daughters may:

- feel that they have failed to carry out their parental responsibility
- fear ostracism by their community or wider family
- feel fearful or guilty about not carrying out what they may believe is a religious obligation
- worry about not being able to find suitable husbands for their daughters, which remains a real concern, as was highlighted in a study of Somali men which indicated that one third would prefer a circumcised wife, and almost three quarters of their parents

would want them to have a circumcised wife
(Williams, 1998).

This shows how crucial it is for professionals to be aware of and
understand the cultural context around female circumcision, in order
to appreciate the predicament of those that support the practice.

*How should professionals deal with physical, psychological
and emotional distress in older women?*

1 Older women may be more reluctant to seek help for
   gynaecological problems because of embarrassment and fears
   about the attitudes of professionals. As such, they may endure
   problems for as long as they can. Professionals should therefore
   make every effort to make women feel as comfortable as possible
   to build confidence and trust.

2 Professionals should be careful when explaining to women any
   links between their circumcision and presenting problems. Whilst
   this is necessary, it needs to be done very sensitively, as it is more
   likely to evoke a defensive reaction or resentment.

3 If there is evidence of any psychological distress, this should be
   explored and, where appropriate, referrals made to more specialised
   services. Bearing in mind the taboos around mental health and
   psychological issues (which are likely to be more stringent within
   this age group), it may be more appropriate to explore and inform
   women about alternative support systems, which may be more
   acceptable and beneficial. It is important, therefore, for professionals
   to familiarise themselves with voluntary local and national
   organisations, such as African women's groups etc., who may be able
   to provide support and advice to women.

IV Working with families

Family background

Many of the 'perpetrators' of FGM in this country are not evil
individuals intent on hurting their children but are, on the contrary,
families who genuinely have their child's best interests at heart.
Nevertheless, in the UK the practice is outlawed and all professionals
coming into contact with the practice have a legal responsibility to act
in accordance with the law.

In theory it is a very clear-cut matter, but in practice, professionals
struggle to work with families around this issue. Many are refugee
families who may well have had very difficult experiences, including:

- exposure to war and violence
- poverty, malnutrition, illness, assault, physical injury
- experience of chaos, instability, unpredictability
- witnessing death, dead bodies, injury to others
- separation from parents, children or other family members
- deprived schooling, health care, and social services
- loss of family members, friends, home, neighbourhood, childhood.
- loss of trust and confidence in people

Research has shown very high rates of mental health problems within refugee communities secondary to their life experiences. In addition, many will be struggling to adapt to a radically different culture where there may have to contend with:

- role-reversal or ambiguity of family roles, e.g. other (female) members of the family forced to look for work; children being relied upon to communicate with the outside world because of language difficulties
- bad news from country of origin where there may be ongoing wars and/or natural disasters
- experiences of racism or discrimination
- immigration issues, family reunification or reconfiguration
- socio-economic stresses: poverty, unemployment and poor housing in deprived areas, where crime may be rife
- social isolation, particularly with government initiatives to disperse refugees around the country
- family difficulties around cross-cultural conflict, with children wanting to adapt new ways which threaten family values and beliefs

Within this context, families may desperately cling to predictable cultural and religious practices that are their only source of security and stability.

Understanding family roles
It is essential also to bear in mind the importance of the extended family system that is likely to be operating within these communities. Understanding the roles of various family members will also be important when working with families and, though not set in stone, the following roles are common to many families:

Mothers

- may have a passive role in decision-making for themselves and their children
- may genuinely wish to uphold the practice of female circumcision or feel compelled to do so out of fear of ostracism from their family or the wider community.
- may themselves face distress and anxiety as they become aware of their own physical and psychological difficulties as having been caused by their circumcision.

Fathers

- are often the primary decision-makers
- may genuinely wish to protect their daughters from circumcision, or see non-circumcision as putting their honour at stake, and fear loss of respect in the community
- may worry about the consequences of not circumcising their daughters and losing control over them, particularly in western societies where promiscuity is not actively discouraged
- may not feel happy to discuss such intimate issues with female health professionals
- may feel overwhelmed, anxious, angry, very scared and unable to vent these feelings

Older women (grandmothers, paternal/maternal aunts)

- are much respected in the family structure and consulted on important decisions
- are often the ones that push for the circumcision to happen
- their status in the community is very important and often measured by the extent of their adherence to cultural, traditional and religious practices

Professional dilemmas

Professionals may need to get involved with families when suspecting a girl is at risk of being circumcised (child protection issue); finding out that a girl has been circumcised and has younger sisters who may be at risk (child protection issue); seeking a referral for counselling/therapy following concerns about psychological, emotional, or behavioural problems that may be secondary to circumcision; when girls under the age of consent are requesting a reversal operation in the absence of parental consent.

These four scenarios will be looked at individually, and guidance will be provided for each case.

Suspecting a girl is at risk of being circumcised

How might this come to light?

- the health visitor may have concerns
- teachers at school may hear a child talking about seeing an older sister/cousin being circumcised
- a child may mention she is going on holiday to have a big ceremony
- friends or relatives may alert professionals

What should professionals do?

1   Professionals who have concerns about children at risk of FGM need to take all reports seriously and consult ACPC guidelines and contact social services as the lead agency in child protection matters.

2   Social services should initiate a section 47 investigation, whilst taking account of the following:

a) families are likely to feel threatened by a group of all white professionals; efforts should be made wherever possible, therefore, to include professionals *either* from the same ethnic background as the family, *or* the same religious background, *or* from a minority ethnic background. Professionals held in high esteem such as doctors and nurses, may also have more influence and should also be considered when meetings are being convened.

b) removal of the child should always be as a last resort, and social workers should not assume that parents and families are aware of the legal situation or understand the links between FGM and child protection issues.

c) be aware of the greater impact that can be had with families by having a prior understanding of the historical and cultural basis to FGM. Listen patiently to their concerns and views, however passionate. Many may voice concerns about cultural norms, community ostracism and future problems in marrying their daughters if they remain uncircumcised. It is very important that professionals acknowledge and empathise with these dilemmas, as these are very real issues facing communities. To dismiss, disregard or attack them or the culture, will therefore lead to resistance and a reluctance to heed advice. Instead, professionals need to convey their understanding, but point out the law and the dangers to health.

d) most families are unlikely to be confrontational and ultimately will want the best for their child. By pitching information in a way that families can relate to i.e. by focusing on the negative health effects, such as the possibility of infertility and other aspects likely to strike a chord with families (in addition to legislation), families are more likely to listen and take notice. A major influence would be the support of a respected community or religious figure.

e) ensure interpreters are available if necessary

3 Further advice on dealing with situations can be obtained from FORWARD.

Finding out that a girl has been circumcised and has younger sisters who may be at risk

How might this come to light?

- GP observation during examination of child
- children mentioning to teachers /school nurses that they have been circumcised
- teachers observing sudden psychological/emotional/ behavioural changes at school
- children disclosing concerns about a younger sibling
- relatives/friends alerting professionals

What should professionals do?

1 Professionals should follow ACPC guidelines as above.

2 Guidelines from the previous section should also be followed with regards to engaging and working with families.

Seeking a referral to the Child and Adolescent Mental Health Services Team (CAMHS)

How might this come to light?

- from teacher observations and concerns about behaviour
- school doctors or school nurse observations
- parental concerns discussed with GPs or teachers

What should professionals do?

1   On suspecting that a child has been subject to FGM, the usual steps for child protection will need to be followed by social services.

2   Following this, if there are concerns at school about behavioural or emotional issues, teachers should deal with it as they would with concerns about any other child displaying emotional or behavioural problems, i.e. by inviting parents to a meeting to discuss these concerns.

3   Do not assume that parents will understand the possible link between FGM and behavioural or emotional problems and that they will, therefore, raise it as a potential precipitating factor.

4   Bear in mind the taboos around emotional and psychological problems and try to talk about concerns in a way that is meaningful to them (i.e. in relation to health and well-being or concentration levels/performance at school, rather than using terms such as anxiety or depression). Explain who might be able to offer help, how, and where.

5   Mental health professionals (clinical psychologists, psychiatrists etc.) should, where appropriate, ask questions about FGM as part of their assessment, so as to inform their understanding and formulation of the problem. Where FGM is found to have been carried out and where psychological symptoms are found to be secondary to this, this should be explained to parents and the opportunity should once again be used to educate parents about legislation, negative health effects, etc. Professionals should be mindful that parents may themselves need help and support in coming to terms with feelings of guilt that may arise as they become aware of the negative repercussions FGM has had on their child.

Girls under the age of consent requesting a reversal operation

How might this come to light?

-   Girls may make requests through school doctors, school nurses, teachers, GPs or family planning clinics

What should professionals do?

1   In the UK, everyone has the power to exercise their rights – and in some circumstances, even when under the age of consent, provided they are found to be competent in accordance with the Fraser (Gillick) competency test. Lord Scarman (1986) has defined this as:

> *the attainment by a child of sufficient discretion to enable*
> *him/her to exercise a wise choice in his/her own interests*
>
> Gillick, 1986

This is measured against a number of different criteria including chronological age, and level of maturation.

2 Providing a child meets the criteria which deems her Gillick competent, she is able to request a reversal operation without parental consent. In such circumstances professionals should find out her reasons for wanting to have this carried out (just as they would in other cases). Bearing in mind the cultural complexities around FGM and the crucial role of the family in decision making, without deterring her from having this procedure done, professionals should encourage her to consider the potential long-term implications for her future of not informing parents of her decision, and talk through these issues.

3 Girls should be referred to counsellors proficiently trained in the area of FGM who have an understanding of the cultural issues, bearing in mind that a reversal operation will change their anatomy from that which they are used to.

RECOMMENDATIONS

MOST WORK ON 'RACE' AND HEALTH IN BRITAIN has tended to concentrate on the 'external' issues facing minority ethnic groups, such as racism, employment, housing, education etc. Whilst a lot has been achieved, a lot less has been achieved in dealing with the particular 'internal' issues of some groups, such as FGM. One of the recurrent themes in this book has been in relation to the inadequate service provision for circumcised women. The need for the government to take a holistic approach, for health professionals to provide appropriate care, and for local statutory bodies to ensure relevant support services, is critical in light of the number of women who have already been circumcised, and the young girls who are at risk.

The following recommendations are being put forward to help the relevant bodies deal with female circumcision effectively, and promote the well-being of women and girls:

Media

The media can play a key part in raising awareness of the physical and psychological dangers of FGM. However, it has so far sensationalised the stories and, in so doing, demonised the culture of those practising communities. It is recommended that the media:

1 own up to their responsibility to help prevent and stop FGM by raising public awareness within communities, and informing about the physical and psychological dangers.

2 avoid sensationalising stories and demonising other cultures or religions.

3 own up to the responsibility of being a true community media serving *everyone*.

Health and social care

FGM affects the physical, psychological, sexual, and social wellbeing of women and girls. Proactive and preventive measures are required. It is recommended that:

1   the Department of Health set up a team to co-ordinate good practice among relevant agencies. This team should be supported by an Independent Advisory Panel on FGM made up of key religious and community figures, specialists, and activists from the country.

2   the Department of Health should consider running national campaigns on the adverse impact of FGM as well as produce booklets for distribution at relevant nursery schools, and primary schools.

3   all Primary Care Trusts, National Health Service Trusts and other relevant organisations should appoint a named individual on FGM to train GPs, paediatricians, midwives, health visitors, nurses, obstetricians, gynaecologists, and other healthcare professionals and to work with communities to raise awareness of the dangers of FGM and build confidence and provide health care support in individual cases.

4   there should be a co-ordinated and holistic approach to tackling the issue at local level. The local health body should take the lead in ensuring that their Local Strategic Partnership develops a 'multi-agency' plan supported by a measurable action plan on the matter. This would allow for different agencies like social services, education departments and others to pool their resources for effective action.

5   the Department of Health and local statutory bodies should fund local projects that work towards the elimination of FGM and the promotion of the wellbeing of circumcised women and girls, on a long-term basis.

6   the Department of Health should set up a national FGM help line.

Education and training

It is recommended that:

1   the DfES takes a lead in providing funding to LEAs, as well as voluntary community organisations, to set up innovative educational projects in schools and communities, as well as capacity-building projects for women.

2 FGM is incorporated into the core training syllabus for nurses, midwives, health visitors and medical students.

3 specific guidance and training is provided to schools and teachers through specialist materials.

4 the LEA should appoint a named individual with FGM responsibility.

5 staff who deal with child protection issues in schools must undergo full training on FGM.

6 the DfES should include FGM issues in the Sex and Relationship Education Guidance.

Government and legislation

It is recommended that:

1 the government takes a holistic approach to tackling FGM.

2 the government makes a full assessment of local authority provision and guidance on FGM, particularly with reference to child protection.

3 the government ensures that there are effective monitoring procedures in place to identify girls at risk and to identify those that have been taken away to be circumcised.

4 there is effective training, information and guidance to health providers and health care professionals.

5 support mechanisms are available for girls who have suffered from their experience.

6 the government runs a national campaign to communicate the implications of the new law on FGM.

7 appropriate funding and support is provided to those NGOs working towards the elimination of FGM and the promotion of women's wellbeing.

Research

It is recommended that:

1 the government collates regular research information on the prevalence, ethnic make-up and perceptions, experiences and views of people on the practice of FGM.

2 the government incorporates data into mainstream policy papers, e.g. the UK Sexual Health Strategy; the Children at Risk Green Paper.

3   research into local service provision and inter-agency co-operation and collaboration is required to map out needs and test the effectiveness of local services.

4   research institutions pay particular attention to this area of research. Whilst there are volumes of both academic and non-academic material on other groups, very little is known about FGM-practising communities, such as the Somali and Sudanese communities in Britain.

Community organisations

It is recommended that:

1   the government provides appropriate sustainable long-term funding to local community organisations to help in their long-term planning and programmes.

2   funding should be available for local strategic partnerships (LSPs) to establish a local FGM advisory board, made up of local religious and community figures. All the evidence suggests that communities are more likely to listen to religious figures assuring them that female circumcision is not a religious requirement.

3   the government recognises the positive contribution of community organisations and activists through local/national awards schemes.

4   community organisations need to help educate as well as build the capacity and confidence of girls and women.

GLOSSARY OF ABBREVIATIONS

ACPC	Area Child Protection Committees
AH	Anno Hegirae – the emigration of the Prophet Muhammad (pbuh), from Mecca to Medina in AD 622. The event marks the start of the Islamic era and of the Islamic calendar.
APPG	All-Party Parliamentary Group
BMA	British Medical Association
CAMHS	Child and Adolescent Mental Health Services
CAMS	Commission Internationals pour l'Abolition des Mutilations Sexuelle
CEDAW	Convention on the Elimination of all forms of Discrimination Against Women
CRC	Convention on the Rights of the Child
DfEE	Department for Education and Employment
DfES	Department for Education and Skills
DHS	Demographic Health Survey
DoH	Department of Health
DSM	Diagnostic and Statistical Manual of Mental Disorders
EWO	Education Welfare Officer
FORWARD	Foundation for Women's Health Research and Development
GMC	General Medical Council
IAC	Inter-African Committee on Traditional Practices
ICESCR	International Covenant on Economic, Social and Cultural Rights
LA	Local Authority
LBWHAP	London Black Women's Health Action Project
LSPs	Local Strategic Partnerships
MRG	Minority Rights Group
NGO	Non Governmental Organisation
NHS	National Health Service
OAU	Organisation of African Unity
PCT	Primary Care Trusts
PTSD	Post-Traumatic Stress Disorder
RCM	Royal College of Midwives
RCN	Royal College of Nursing
RCOG	Royal College of Obstetricians and Gynaecologists
UN	United Nations
UNESCO	United Nations Education Scientific and Cultural Organisation
UNFPA	United Nations Population Fund
UNIFEM	United Nations Agencies for Women
UNICEF	United Nations Children's Fund
WHO	World Health Organisation

BIBLIOGRAPHY

Abraham, L and Wolbarst, M D (1932), 'Circumcision and Penile Cancer', *Lancet*, January 16, pp 150-153

Abu-Bakr (1985), 'Circumcision and infibulation', *Middle East, vol 6,* pp 624-631

Abu Dawood's *anthology of authentic hadith*, Muhammad Naser al-Din al-Albani (ed.) (1409, AH), Arab Office of Education

Abu Dawood's *Sunas*, Muhammad Muhyi al-din Abd al-Hamid (ed.) (1354, AH), Egypt: Mustafa Muhammad's Press

Addis Ababa Declaration, The (1997), Organisation of African Unity (OAU) document

African (Banjul) Charter on Human and People's Rights (1981), Organisation of African Unity (OAU)

African charter on human and people's rights, The (1997), Organisation of African Unity (OAU) document

Al-Awwa, M S (1994) 'Islamic Ruling on Male and Female Circumcision Female Circumcision Neither a Sunna, nor a Sign of Respect', Egypt: WHO

Ali, M M (1996), *The Washington Report on Middle East Affairs*, May-June, p.13: Washington D.C.

American Psychiatric Association (1994), *'Diagnostic and Statistical Manual of Mental Disorders'*, 4th ed, Washington: APA

Amnesty International (1998), *Female Genital Mutilation: a human rights information pack*, London: Amnesty International

Anwar, M, and Bakhsh, Q (2003), *British Muslims and State Policies*, Coventry: Centre for Research in Ethnic Relations, University of Warwick

Anwar, M (1993), *Muslims in Britain: 1991 Census and Other Statistical Sources*, Coventry: Centre for Research in Ethnic Relations, University of Warwick

Arbesman, M, Kahler, L and Buck, G M (1993), 'Assessment of the impact of female circumcision on the Gynaecological Genitourinary and Obstetrical health problems of women from Somalia: literature review and case series', *Women and Health*, vol 20, no 3, pp 27-42

Asefa, S (1994), *Unacknowledged Acts of Violence in the Name of Tradition, Religion and Social Imperative*. Interpersonal Violence, Health and Gender Politics, 2nd ed, Stanley French: Brown Communications: Dubuque and Ottawa

Assaad, M B (1979), *Female circumcision in Egypt: current research and social implications*, Cairo: American University

Azmi, Qamaruzzaman Maulana (2003), interview on 7 June 2003, Manchester

Azmi, Qamaruzzaman Maulana (1994), quoted in Lewis, P (ed.) *Islamic Britain*, London: Tauris

Al-Baihaqi, Abu-Bakr Ahmad Ibn-al-Husayn (died 1066) (1991), *Ma'rifat al-sunan wal-athar, Jami'at al-dirasat al-islamiyyah:* Karachi

Ballard, C, Stanley, A, and Brockington, I (1995), 'PTSD after childbirth', *British Journal of Psychiatry*, vol 166, pp 525-528

Banjul Declaration, The (1998),African Commission on Human and People's Rights, Banjul: Gambia

Banton, M (1955), *The Colored Quarter*, London: Oxford University Press

Barker, P (1988), *Basic Child Psychiatry* (5th Edition), Great Britain: Blackwell Scientific Publication

Barker-Benfield, G (1976), *The Horrors of the Half-Known Life: Male Attitudes Toward Women and Sexuality in Nineteenth-Century America*, New York: Harper and Row

Basher, T A (1982), *Psychosocial aspects of female circumcision*, WHO/EMRO Technical Publications, no 2, WHO

Basher, T A (1977), 'Psychological aspects of female circumcision', in *Traditional practices affecting the health of women*: report of a seminar, WHO/EMRO (1979), publication, no 2, WHO

Beech, A B & Robinson, J (1985), 'Nightmares following childbirth', *British Journal of Psychiatry*, 131, pp 981-986

Beijing declaration and platform for action (Beijing +5)(1995), United Nations

Bilotti, E (2000), *The Practice of FGM*, USA: Lexington, MA

Bitschai, J (1956), *A History of Urology in Egypt*, Cambridge: Riverside Press

Blake, D D, Weathers, F W, Nagy, L M, Kaloupek, D G, Klauminzer, G, Charney, D S and Keane, T M (1990), 'A clinician rating scale for assessing current and lifetime PTSD: The CAPS-1', *Behaviour Therapist*, vol 13, pp 187-88

Boddy, J (1982), 'Womb as oasis: the symbolic context of pharaonic circumcision in rural Northern Sudan', *American Ethnologist*, vol 9, pp 682-698

Breslau, N, Davis, G C, Andreski, P, and Peterson, E (1991) 'Traumatic events and post-traumatic stress disorder in an urban population of young adults', *Archives of General Psychiatry*, 48, pp 216-222

Breslau, N, and Davis, G C (1987) 'Post-traumatic stress disorder: the stressor criterion'. *The Journal of Nervous and Mental Disease*, 158, (6), pp 440-445

British Medical Association (1997), *Access to Healthcare for Asylum Seekers*, London: BMA

British Medical Association (1996), *Female Genital Mutilation: Caring for Patients and Child Protection*, revised 2001, London: BMA

Brown, Y, Calder, B, and Rae, D (1989), 'Female circumcision', *Canadian Nurse*, vol 85, pp 19-22

Bukhari's *anthology of authentic hadith*, (published together with Ibn Hajar's *Fath al-bari*), Egypt: A1-Salafiyah Press, (1380 AH)

Burstyn, L (1995), 'Female Circumcision comes to America', *The Atlantic Monthly*, October, pp 28-35

Convention on the Elimination of all forms of Discrimination Against Women (1992), United Nations

Convention on the Rights of the Child (CRC) (1990), United Nations

Daly, C (1950), 'The psychobiological origins of circumcision', *International Journal of Psychoanalysis*, vol XXX1, part 4, pp 217-236

Dawood, A (1996), 'Pharaonic Circumcision (infibulation)', in Sabbagh, L M (ed), *Islamic Ruling on Male and Female Circumcision*, Egypt, WHO

De Villeneuve, A (1937), 'Etude sur une coutume Somalie: Les femmes consues', *Journal de la Societe des Africainistes*, vol 7, no 1, pp 15-32

Declaration of the rights of the child (1959), United Nations

Demographic and Health Survey (DHS) (1999), Burkina Faso

Demographic and Health Survey (DHS)(1994), Central African Republic

emographic and Health Survey (DHS)(2000), Egypt

Demographic and Health Survey (DHS)(1997), Eritria

Demographic and Health Survey (DHS)(1999), Guinea

Demographic and Health Survey (DHS)(1999), Ivory Coast

Demographic Survey Somalia (1999), CARE International

Department of Health (2003) *Equalities and Diversity Strategy*. unpublished internal document, HR Department, London: DoH

Department of Health (1998), *Experiences, Attitudes and Beliefs of Young Single Somalis living in London*, London: HMSO

Department of Health (1991) *Working Together under the Children Act 1989: a guide to arrangements for inter-agency co-operation for the protection of children from abuse*. London: HMSO

DeWolfe, D (2001), *Mental Health Response to Mass Violence and Terrorism: a training manual for mental health workers and human service workers*, USA: National Centre for PTSD

DfEE (2000), *Sex and relationships guidance*, London: HMSO

Ehrenreich, B, and English, Deidre (1973), *Complaints and Disorders*, New York: The Feminist Press

El-Dareer, A (1983a), 'Attitudes of Sudanese people to the practice of female circumcision', *International Journal of Epidemiology*, vol 12, pp 138-44

El-Dareer, A (1983b), 'Epidemiology of female circumcision in the Sudan', *Tropical Doctor*, vol 13, pp 41-45

El-Dareer, A (1982), *Women: Why do you Weep?*, Zed Press

European Monitoring Centre on Racism and Xenophobia (EUMC) (October 2001), *Anti- Islamic Reactions in the EU after the Terrorist Acts against the USA*, Vienna: EUMC

Feibelman, P (1997) 'Natural Causes', *Double Take Magazine*, Winter ed

Focus Group A (2002), 9 November 2002, Manchester

Focus Group B (2003), 26 April 2003, Manchester

Focus Group C (2003), 24 May 2003, Birmingham

Focus Group D (2003), 20 June 2003, London

Foundation for Women's Health Research and Development (FORWARD) (1998), *Out of Sight, Out of Mind?: The Report of a Survey into Inter-Agency Policies and Procedures relating to Female Genital Mutilation (FGM) in England and Wales*, London: FORWARD

Gallo, P (1988) 'Female circumcision in Somalia', *Mankind Quarterly*, 29, pp

165-180

Gellis, S S (1978), 'Circumcision', *American Journal of Diseases of Childhood, vol 132, pp 1168*

Gillan, C (2003), Debate on proposed FGM Bill, 21 March 2003, House of Commons: London

Gillick vs West Norfolk and Wisbech Health Authority (1986), AC 112

Green, B L, Wilson, J P, & Lindy, J (1985) 'A conceptual framework for post-traumatic stress syndrome among survivor groups' in C. R. Figley (ed). *Trauma and its Wake: The study and Treatment of Post-Traumatic Stress Disorder*, New York: Brunner/Mazel

Harden, B (1985) 'Female Circumcision: A Norm in Africa', *International Herald Tribune, Washington Post Source*, 29 July 1985.

Hastings, J, (ed) (1928) *Encyclopedia of Religion and Ethics. (vol 3)* New York, NY: Charles Scribner and Sons

Hathout, H.M (1963), 'Some aspects of female circumcision', *British Journal of Obstetrics and Gynaecology*, vol 70, pp 505-7

Hedley, R, and Dorkenoo, E (1992), *Child Protection and Female Genital Mutilation: Advice for Health, Education and Social Work Professionals*, London: FORWARD

Helzer, J E, Robins, L N, and McEvoy, L (1987) 'Post-traumatic stress disorder in the generalpopulation: Findings of the epidemiological catchment area survey', *New England Journal of Medicine*, 317, pp 1630-1634

Herman, J L (1992) 'Complex PTSD: a syndrome in survivors of prolonged and reported trauma', *Journal of Traumatic Stress*, 5, 377-392

Hillas, S & Cox, T (1987) *Post-Traumatic Stress Disorder in the Police*, Occasional paper. London: Police Scientific Research and Development Branch, Home Office

HMSO (2003) *Race Relations Amendment Act (2000)*, London: HMSO

Hobfoll, S and Leiberman, J R (1987) 'Personality and social resources in immediate and continued stress resistance among women', *Journal of Personality and Social Psychology*, 52, pp 18-26

Holsti, O (1969) *Contents Analysis for the Social Sciences and Humanities*, Addison-Wesley Publishing Company

Home Office Statistical Bulletin (1998) *Asylum Statistics United Kingdom* 1997, London: Home Office, Issue 14

Home Office Statistical Bulletin (1998) *Control of Immigration: Statistics United Kingdom, Second Half and Year 1997*, London: Home Office, Issue 13

Horowitz, M J, Wilner, N, and Alvarez, W (1979) 'Impact of Event Scale: A Measure of Subjective Stress', *Psychosomatic Medicine*, 41, (3), pp 209-218

Hosken, Fran (1995), *Stop Female Genital Mutilation: Women Speak: Facts and Actions*, Women's International Network News, USA: Lexington, MA

Hosken, Fran (1994), *The Hosken Report*, 4th edn., Women's International Network News, USA: Lexington, MA

Hosken, F (1978), ''The Epidemiology of FGM', *Tropical Doctor, vol 8,* pp 150-156

Hunt, Lord (2000) *Parliamentary Debate on 21 March 2003,* London: House of Lords

Ibn Hajar's *Taqrib al-tahthib* in Muhammad Awadah (ed.) (1406 AH), Beirut: Dar al-Bashayer al-Islamiyah

Ibn Hajar's *Fath al-bari* in Al-Salafiyah Press Publication (1380 AH.), Egypt

Ibn Hajar's *Tahthib al-tahthib* in Haydar Abad al-Dukun Publications (1325 AH)

Ibn Maja's *Anthology of authentic hadith* in Muhammad Naser al-Albani al-Din (ed.) (2nd ed.) (1408 AH), Arab Office of Education

Ibn Maja's *Sunnan,* in Muhammad Fuad Abd al-Baqi (ed.) (1372 AH), Egypt: Dar Ihya al-Kutub al-Arabiyya

Inter-African Committee on Traditional Practices Affecting the Health of Women and Children (IAC) (1992), *Survey on the practice of FGM in Benin,* Benin: IAC

International Covenant on Civil and Political Rights (1960), Geneva: Office of the High Commissioner for Human Rights

International Covenant on Economic, Social and Cultural Rights (1976), Geneva: United Nations Publications

Al-Iraqi, Zein al-Din, (died 1404), *Kitab tarh al-tathrib fi sharh al-taqrib,* Beirut: Dar ihya' al-turath al-arabi

Jacobs, M A, Spilken, A Z and Norman, M M (1969) 'The relationship between life change, maladaptive aggression and URI in male college students' *Psychosomatic Medicine,* 31, pp 31-44

Jordan, J A (1994), 'Female genital mutilation (female circumcision)', *British Journal of Obstetrics and Gynaecology,* vol 101, pp 94-95

Kennedy, J G (1970), 'Circumcision and Excision in Egyptian Nubia', *Man,* New Series, vol 5, no 2, pp175-199

Kensington, Chelsea and Westminster (KCW) Health Authority (1999), *It's for us to decide,* London: KCWHA

Kenyatta, J (1953), *Facing Mount Kenya,* London: Secker and Warburg

Khalifa, N K (1994), 'Reasons behind practising recircumcision among educated Sudanese women', *Ahfad Journal,* vol 22, no 2, pp 16-33

Killingray, D (1994), *Africans in Britain,* Frank Publishers

Koso-Thomas, O (1987), *The Circumcision of Women. A Strategy for Eradication,* London: Zed Books

Kwateng-Kluvitse (2003), Interview March 2003

Lantier, J (1972), *La cite Magique,* Editions Fayard

Lightfoot-Klein, H, and Shaw, E (1991), 'Special needs of ritually circumcised women patients', *Journal of Obstetric gynaecological neonatal nursing,* vol 20, no 2, pp 102-3

Lightfoot-Klein, H (1990), 'Rites of purification and their effects: some psychological aspects of female genital circumcision and infibulation (pharaonic circumcision) in an Afro-Arab Islamic society (Sudan)', *Journal of Psychology and Human Sexuality,* vol 2, no 2, pp 79-91

Lightfoot-Klein, H (1989a), 'The sexual experience and marital adjustment of genitally circumcised and infibulated females in the Sudan', *The Journal of Sex Research*, vol 26, no 3, pp 375-392

Lightfoot-Klein, H (1989b), *Prisoners of ritual: an odyssey into female genital circumcision in Africa*, New York

Little, K (1992), 'Circumcision: pros and cons', *Modern Medicine*, no 37, September ed

Lockhat, H (1999a), *A preliminary investigation of the psychological effects of female circumcision (female genital mutilation)*, unpublished Doctorate in Clinical Psychology Thesis, Faculty of Medicine, University of Manchester

Lockhat, H (1999b), in *The Road to Change*, WHO Training video, Geneva: WHO

MacPherson, W (1999), *The Stephen Lawrence Inquiry Report*, London: HMSO

Mahran, M (1981), 'Medical dangers of female circumcision', *IPPF, Medical Bulletin*, vol 15, no2

McCafferty, C (2003), *Debate on proposed FGM Bill*, 21 March 2003, London: House of Commons

McCaffery, M (1995), 'Female genital mutilation: consequences for reproductive and sexual health', *Sexual and Marital Therapy*, vol 10, no2, pp189-200

Minority Rights Group (1996) (revised ed.), *Female genital mutilation: proposals for change*, London: MRG

Modawi, S (1974), 'The Impact of Social and Economic Changes in Female Circumcision', *Sudan Medical Association Congress Series, no1,* Sudan Medical Association, Khartoum

Mohamed, Z (2003), *Interview on 7 March*, 2003, Manchester

Muslim's *anthology of authentic hadith* in Muhammad Fuad Abd al-Baqi (ed.), the Istanbul edition

Mustafa, S (1966), 'Female circumcision and infibulation in the Sudan'. *Journal of obstetrics and Gynaecology of the British Commonwealth, vol 73, pp 302-306*

Myers, R A, Isenalumhe, A E, Akenzua, G I, and Omorodian, F I (1985), 'Circumcision: its nature and practice among some ethnic groups in southern Nigeria', *Social Science and Medicine*, vol 21, no 5, pp 588

Nayra, A (1982), *Khul-khalla: Five Egyptian women tell their stories*, New York: Syracuse University Press

Ntiri, D (1993), 'Circumcision and health among rural women of southern Somalia as part of a family life survey', *Health Care for women International*, vol 14, no 3, pp 219-220

Omen, E W (1983), *Genital Mutilation: Every woman's problem*. Working Paper no 22, in *working papers on women in international development*, East Lansing, MI: Michigan State University

ONS (2003), *Census 2001,* London: HMSO

Pridie, E, Lorenzen, A, Cruickshank, A, Hovell, J, MacDonald, D, Bedri, A, Halim Mohamed, A, Abu Shamma, A, and El Mahl, E (1945), *Female circumcision in the Anglo-Egyptian Sudan,* Oxford: Bodleian Library

Prohibition of Female Circumcision Act (1985), London: HMSO

Pynoos, R, and Nader, K (1993), 'Issues in the treatment of post-traumatic stress in children and adolescents', in Wilson, J P, and Rapheal, B, eds, *International Handbook of Traumatic Stress Syndromes,* New York: Plenum

Read, D (1998) Out of Sight, Out of Mind?, London: FORWARD

Remondino, P C (1974), *History of Circumcision from the Earliest Times to the Present,* New York: AMS Press, (original work published 1891)

Roe, M (2003), *Debate on proposed FGM Bill,* 21 March 2003, London: House of Commons

Royal College of Midwives (RCM) (1998), *Position paper 21,* London: RCM

Royal College of Obstetricians and Gynaecologists (RCOG) (2003), *Female Genital Mutilation: Statement no 3,* May 2003

Royal College of Obstetricians and Gynaecologists (RCOG) (1997), *Female Circumcision (Female Genital Mutilation),* press release, June 1997

Royal College of Nursing (RCN) (1996), *FGM: The unspoken issue,* London: RCN

Al-Sabbagh, M L (1996), 'The Right Path to Health' in *Islamic Ruling on Male and Female Circumcision,* Egypt: World Health Organisation

Sabeq, S Sunnas jurisprudence. Beirut: Dar al-Kitab al-Arabi

Schoen, E J (1990), 'The status of circumcision of newborns', *New England Journal of Medicine,* vol 322, pp 1308-1312

Scott, M and Stradling, S (1994) 'PTSD without the trauma.' *British Journal of Clinical Psychology.* 33, 71-74

Scott, M and Stradling, S (1992) *Counselling for Post-Traumatic Stress Disorder.* London: Sage

Sequeira, J H (1931), 'Female circumcision and infibulation of females', *Lancet, vol 2,* pp 1054-6

Shandall, A (1967), 'Female circumcision and infibulation of females', *Sudan Medical Journal,* no 5, pp 178-211

Shaw, E (1985), 'Female circumcision', *American Journal of Nursing,* vol 85, pp 684-87

Shweder, Richard A (2000), 'What About Female Genital Mutilation? And Why Understanding Culture Matters in the First Place', *Daedalus,* vol 129, pp 209-232

Slack, A (1988), 'Female Circumcision: A Critical Appraisal', *Human Rights Quarterly,* vol 10, pp 437-486

Sudan National Committee on Traditional Practices (SNCTP) and Save the Children Sweden (1996), *Survey on practice rates of FGM in Sudan,* Sudan: SNCTP & SCS

Sudanese Family Planning Association (SFPA)(1975), Happy Family, Sudan: SFPA

Tanner, T (1866), 'On excision of the clitoris as a cure for hysteria', *Tr Obstetric Society London,* VIII, pp 360-384

Thiam, A (1978), *La Parole aux negresses,* Paris

Al-Tirmithi's *Sunnan* in Al-ahwathi's masterpiece (ed.) (1343 AH), India

Toubia, N (1994), 'Female circumcision as a public health issue' *The New England Journal of Medicine*, vol 33, pp 712-716

Toubia, N (1993), *Female Genital Mutilation:A Call for Global Action*, New York: Women Ink

UNICEF (1980) Position of UNICEF on Female Excision, Department of Information

United Nations International Conference on Population and Development (1994), *Programme of Action of the Conference*, Geneva: United Nations Publications

United Nations (September 1985) *Traditional practices affecting the health of women and children*, UN Doc ECN.4./HC.42/1985/L5, 12 September 1985

Universal Declaration of Human Rights (1948), Geneva: WHO

Vertoved, S, and Peach, C, eds (1997), *Islam in Europe: the politics of religion and community*, Basingstoke: Macmillan

Verzin, J A (1975), 'Sequelae of female circumcision', *Tropical Doctor*, vol 5, pp 163-169

Vienna Declaration and Programme of Action (1993), Geneva: Office of the United Nations High Commissioner for Human Rights

Viva (1978), 'The silence over FGM in Kenya', in *Viva magazine*

Wallerstein, E (1980), *Circumcision:An American health fallacy*, New York: Springer Publishing Company

Williams et al (1998), *Experiences, Attitudes and Beliefs of Young Somalians Living in London*, London: London School of Hygiene and Tropical Medicine/London Black Women's Health Action Project

Wolbarst, A L (1932), *Circumcision and Penile Cancer*, 1: pp 150-153

Women's National Commission (1997), *Growing up Female in the UK*, London: HMSO

Woodlard, D and Edwards, R M (1997), 'Female circumcision an emerging concern in college health care', *Journal of the American College of Health*, vol 45, no 5, pp 230-232

World Health Organisation (1999), *The Road to Change*, Training video, WHO

World Health Organisation (1998a), *Female Genital Mutilation: an overview*, Geneva: WHO

World Health Organisation (1998b), *A systematic review of health complications following female genital mutilation including sequelae in childbirth* (in press) Geneva: WHO

World Health Organisation (1997), *Female genital mutilation:A Joint WHO/UNICEF/UNFPA Statement*, Geneva: WHO

World Health Organisation (1992), *The International Classification of Mental and Behavioural Disorders (ICD-10)*, Geneva: WHO

World Health Organisation (1989), *Resolution of the Regulatory Committee for Africa*, 39th session, AFR/RC39/129

Wrana, P (1939), 'Historical review: Circumcision' *Archives of Paediatrics*, vol 6

LIST OF USEFUL RESOURCES

Hospitals offering specialist FGM (Female Genital Mutilation) services

African Well Women's Clinic
Guy's and St Thomas Hospital
McNair Centre
London SE1 9RT
Tel: 020 7955 2381
Pager: 020 8345 6789 (881018)
Open: Mon-Fri 9.30am – 4.30pm
Contact: Comfort Momoh

African Well Women's Clinic
Antenatal Clinic
Central Middlesex Hospital
Acton Lane
Park Royal
London NW10 7NS
Tel: 020 8453 2106
Open: Thursday 9.00am – 12.00pm
Contact: Harry Gordon

African Well Women's Clinic
Antenatal Clinic
Northwick Park & St Mark's Hospitals
Watford Road
Harrow
Middlesex HA1 3UJ
Tel: 020 8869 2870
Open: Friday 9.00am – 2.30pm
Contact: Dr Louca

African Well Women's Clinic
Community Health Project
The Refugee Advice Centre
Voucher Administration Scheme
340 High Road
Leyton E10
Tel: 020 8556 1088
Open: Thurs 10.00am – 1.00pm
Contact: Jennifer Bourne

African Women's Health Clinic
Whittington Hospital
London NW10 7NS
Tel: 020 7288 3482
Open: Last Wednesday of each month
(afternoon only)
Contacts: Joy Clark & Georgina Sosa

St Mary's Hospital
Gynaecology & Midwifery Depts
Praed Street
London W2
Tel: 020 7886 6666

Women's and Young People's Service
Sylvia Pinehurst Health Centre
Mile End Hospital
Bancroft Road
London E1 4DG
Tel: 020 7377 7870
Open: Mon-Fri 9.00am – 5.00pm
Contact: Gita Subramanian

African Women's Clinic
The Elizabeth Garrett Anderson
and Obstetric Hospital
Huntley Street
London, WC1E 6DH
Tel: 020 7380 9773
email: egappts@uclh.nhs.uk
Contact: Maligaye Bikoo

Multi-Cultural Antenatal Clinic
Liverpool Women's Hospital
Crown Street
Liverpool L8 7SS
Tel: 0151 708 9988
Open: Mon 5.30-7pm
Thurs 5.30 – 7.00pm
Contact: Dorcas Akeju

African Women's Clinic
Women and Health
4 Carol Street (Camden)
London NW1 OHU
Tel: 020 7482 2786
Women can self-refer for services

Chelsea and Westminster Hospital
Gynaecology & Midwifery Departments
369 Fulham Road
London SW10 9NH
Tel: 020 8746 8000

Groups working on FGM issues in the UK:

Black Women's Health and Family
Support
82 Russia Lane
London, E2 9LU
Tel: 020 8980 3503
email: bwhfs@btconnect.com

Foundation for Women's Health
Research and Development
(FORWARD)
Unit 4
465 – 467 Harrow Road
London, NW10 5NY
Tel: 020 8960 4000
email: forward@forwarduk.org.uk

Research, Action and Information
Network for the Bodily Integrity of
Women (RAINBO)
Suite 5a, Queens Studios
121 Salusbury Road
London NW6 6RG
Tel: 020 7625 3400
email: info@rainbo.org

INDEX